TWELVE SERMONS ON THE RESURRECTION

TWELVE SERMONS

ON THE

RESURRECTION

By

C. H. SPURGEON

BAKER BOOK HOUSE
Grand Rapids, Michigan

Reprinted 1968 by
Baker Book House Company

ISBN: 0-8010-7967-5

First printing, October 1968
Second printing, November 1969
Third printing, November 1972
Fourth printing, January 1974
Fifth printing, January 1976
Sixth printing, June 1977
Seventh printing, September 1978
Eighth printing, February 1980
Ninth printing, December 1981

PHOTOLITHOPRINTED BY CUSHING - MALLOY, INC.
ANN ARBOR, MICHIGAN, UNITED STATES OF AMERICA

CONTENTS

I KNOW THAT MY REDEEMER LIVETH

Text.—"For I know that my redeemer liveth, and that he shall
stand at the latter day upon the earth: and though after my skin
worms destroy this body, yet in my flesh shall I see God: whom I
shall see for myself, and mine eyes shall behold, and not another;
though my reins be consumed within me."—Job xix. 25–27.

OUR text deserves our profound attention; its preface would
hardly have been written had not the matter been of the utmost
importance in the judgment of the patriarch who uttered it.
Listen to Job's remarkable desire: "Oh that my words were
now written! oh that they were printed in a book! That they
were graven with an iron pen and lead in the rock for ever!"
Perhaps, hardly aware of the full meaning of the words he was
uttering, yet his holy soul was impressed with a sense of some
weighty revelation concealed within his words; he therefore
desired that it might be recorded in a book; he has had his
desire the Book of books embalms the words of Job. He wished
to have them graven on a rock; cut deep into it with an iron
pen, and then the lines inlaid with lead; or he would have them
engraven, according to the custom of the ancients, upon a sheet
of metal, so that time might not be able to eat out the inscription.
He has not had his desire in that respect, save only that upon
many and many a sepulchre those words of Job stand recorded,
"I know that my redeemer liveth."

It is the opinion of some commentators that Job, in speaking
of the rock here, intended his own rock-hewn sepulchre, and
desired that this might be his epitaph; that it might be cut deep,
so that ages should not wear it out; that when any asked, "Where
does Job sleep?" as soon as they saw the sepulchre of the patriarch
of Uz, they might learn that he died in hope of resurrection,
resting upon a living Redeemer. Whether such a sentence adorned
the portals of Job's last sleeping-place we know not; but certainly
no words could have been more fitly chosen. Should not the
man of patience, the mirror of endurance, the pattern of trust,
bear as his memorial this golden line, which is as full of all the
patience of hope, and hope of patience, as mortal language

can be? Who among us could select a more glorious motto for his last escutcheon?

In discoursing upon these words I shall speak upon three things. First, *let us, with the patriarch, descend into the grave and behold the ravages of death.* Then, with him, *let us look up on high for present consolation.* And, still in his admirable company, let us, in the third place, *anticipate future delights.*

I.   First of all then, with the patriarch of Uz, LET US DESCEND INTO THE SEPULCHRE.

The body has just been divorced from the soul. Friends who loved most tenderly have said—"Bury my dead out of my sight." The body is borne upon the bier and consigned to the silent earth; it is surrounded by the earthworks of death. Death has a host of troops. If the locusts and the caterpillars be God's army, the worms are the army of death. These hungry warriors begin to attack the city of man. They commence with the outworks; they storm the munition, and overturn the walls. The skin, the city wall of manhood, is utterly broken down, and the towers of its glory covered with confusion. How speedily the cruel invaders deface all beauty.   The face gathers blackness; the countenance is defiled with corruption. Those cheeks once fair with youth, and ruddy with health, have fallen in, even as a bowing wall and a tottering fence, those eyes, the windows of the mind whence joy and sorrow looked forth by turns, are now filled up with the dust of death; those lips, the doors of the soul, the gates of Mansoul, are carried away, and the bars thereof are broken. Alas, ye windows of agates and gates of carbuncle, where are ye now? How shall I mourn for thee, O thou captive city, for the mighty men have utterly spoiled thee! Thy neck, once like a tower of ivory, has become as a fallen column; thy nose, so lately comparable to "the tower of Lebanon, which looketh toward Damascus," is as a ruined hovel; and thy head, which towered like Carmel, lies low as the clods of the valley. Where is beauty now? The most lovely cannot be known from the most deformed.

Cruel have ye been, ye warriors of death. The skin is gone. The troops have entered into the town of Mansoul. And now they pursue their work of devastation; the pitiless marauders fall upon the body itself. There are those noble aqueducts, the veins through which the streams of life were wont to flow, these, instead of being rivers of life, have become blocked up with the soil and wastes of death, and now they must be pulled to pieces; not a single relic of them shall be spared.

Dear friends, why should we wish to have it otherwise? Why should we desire to preserve the body when the soul has gone?

Do not seek to avoid what God has purposed; do not look upon it as a gloomy thing. Regard it as a necessity; nay more, view it as the platform of a miracle, the lofty stage of resurrection, since Jesus shall surely raise again from the dead the particles of this body, however divided from one another. We have heard of miracles, but what a miracle is the resurrection! All the miracles of Scripture, yea even those wrought by Christ, are small compared with this. The philosopher says, "How is it possible that God shall hunt out every particle of the human frame?" He can do it: He has but to speak the word, and every single atom, though it may have travelled thousands of leagues, though it may have been blown as dust across the desert, and anon have fallen upon the bosom of the sea, and then have descended into the depths thereof to be cast up on a desolate shore, sucked up by plants, fed on again by beasts, or passed into the fabric of another man,—I say that individual atom shall find its fellows, and the whole company of particles at the trump of the archangel shall travel to their appointed place, and the body, the very body which was laid in the ground, shall rise again.

When the fabric has been absolutely broken up, the tenement all pulled down, ground to pieces, and flung in handfuls to the wind, so that no relic of it is left, yet when Christ stands in the latter days upon the earth, all the structure shall be brought together, bone to his bone—then shall the might of Omnipotence be seen. This is the doctrine of the resurrection, and happy is he who finds no difficulty here, who looks at it as being an impossibility with man but a possibility with God, and lays hold upon the omnipotence of the Most High and says, "Thou sayest it, and it shall be done!" I comprehend Thee not great God; I marvel at Thy purpose to raise my mouldering bones; but I know that Thou dost great wonders, and I am not surprised that Thou shouldst conclude the great drama of Thy creating works here on earth by re-creating the human frame by the same power by which Thou didst bring from the dead the body of Thy Son Jesus Christ, and by that same divine energy which has regenerated human souls in Thine own image.

II. Now, having thus descended into the grave, and seen nothing there but what is loathsome, LET US LOOK UP WITH THE PATRIARCH AND BEHOLD A SUN SHINING WITH PRESENT COMFORT.

"I know," said he, "that my Redeemer liveth." The word "Redeemer" here used, is in the original "goel"—kinsman. The duty of the kinsman, or goel, was this: suppose an Israelite had alienated his estate, as in the case of Naomi and Ruth; suppose a patrimony which had belonged to a family, had passed away through poverty, it was the goel's business, the redeemer's business to pay the price as the next of kin, and to buy back the heritage. Boaz stood in that relation to Ruth.

Now, the body may be looked upon as the heritage of the soul—the soul's small farm, that little plot of earth in which the soul has been wont to walk and delight, as a man walketh in his garden or dwelleth in his house. Now, that becomes alienated. Death, like Ahab, takes away the vineyard from us who are as Naboth; we lose our patrimonial estate; Death sends his troops to take our vineyard and to spoil the vines thereof and ruin it. But we turn round to Death and say, "I know that my Goel liveth, and He will redeem this heritage; I have lost it; thou takest it from me lawfully, O Death, because my sin hath forfeited my right; I have lost my heritage through my own offence, and through that of my first parent Adam; but there lives One who will buy this back."

Brethren, Job could say this of Christ long before He had descended upon earth, "I know that he liveth;" and now that He has ascended up on high, and led captivity captive, surely we may with double emphasis say, "I know that my Goel, my Kinsman liveth, and that he hath paid the price, that I should have back my patrimony, so that in my flesh I shall see God." Yes, my hands, ye are redeemed with blood; bought not with corruptible things, as with silver and gold, but with the precious blood of Christ. Yes, heaving lungs and palpitating heart, ye have been redeemed! He that redeemed the soul to be His altar has also redeemed the body, that it may be a temple for the Holy Ghost. Not even the bones of Joseph can remain in the house of bondage. No smell of the fire of death may pass upon the garments which His holy children have worn in the furnace.

Remember, too, that it was always considered to be the duty of the goel, not merely to redeem by price, but where that failed, to redeem by power. Hence, when Lot was carried away captive by the four kings, Abraham summoned his own hired servants, and the servants of all his friends, and went out against the kings of the East, and brought back Lot and the captives of Sodom. Now, our Lord Jesus Christ, who once has played the kinsman's part by paying the price for us, liveth, and He will redeem us by power. O Death, thou tremblest at this Name! Thou knowest the might of our Kinsman! Against His arm thou canst not stand! Thou didst once meet Him foot to foot in sterm battle, and O Death, thou didst indeed tread upon His heel. He voluntarily submitted to this, or else, O Death, thou hadst no power against Him. But He slew thee, Death, He slew thee! He rifled all thy caskets, took from thee the key of thy castle, burst open the door of thy dungeon; and now, thou knowest, Death, thou hast no power to hold my body; thou mayst set thy slaves to devour it, but thou shalt give it up, and all their spoil must be restored.

Insatiable Death, from thy greedy maw yet shall return the multitudes whom thou hast devoured. Thou shalt be compelled by the Saviour to restore thy captives to the light of day. I think I see Jesus coming with His Father's servants. The chariots of the Lord are twenty thousand, even thousands of angels. Blow ye the trumpet! blow ye the trumpet! Immanuel rides to battle! The Most Mighty in majesty girds on His sword. He comes! He comes to snatch by power, His people's lands from those who have invaded their portion. Oh, how glorious victory! No battle shall there be. He comes, He sees, He conquers. The sound of the trumpet shall be enough; Death shall fly affrighted; and at once from beds of dust and silent clay, to realms of everlasting day the righteous shall arise.

To linger here a moment, there was yet, very conspicuously in the Old Testament, we are informed, a third duty of the goel, which was to avenge the death of his friend. If a person had been slain, the Goel was the avenger of blood; snatching up his sword, he at once pursued the person who had been guilty of bloodshed. So now, let us picture ourselves as being smitten by Death. His arrow has just pierced us to the heart, but in the act of expiring, our lips are able to boast of vengeance, and in the face of the monster we cry, "I know that my Goel liveth." Thou mayst fly, O Death, as rapidly as thou wilt, but no city of refuge can hide thee from him; he will overtake thee; he will lay hold upon thee, O thou skeleton monarch, and he will avenge my blood on thee. I would that I had powers of eloquence to work out this magnificent thought. Chrysostom, or Christmas Evans could picture the flight of the King of Terrors, the pursuit by the Redeemer, the overtaking of the foe, and the slaying of the destroyer. Christ shall certainly avenge Himself on Death for all the injury which Death hath done to His beloved kinsmen. Comfort thyself then, O Christian; thou hast ever living, even when thou diest, One who avenges thee, One who has paid the price for thee, and One whose strong arms shall yet set thee free.

Passing on in our text to notice the next word, it seems that Job found consolation not only in the fact that he had a Goel, a Redeemer, but that this Redeemer liveth. He does not say, "I know that my Goel *shall live*, but that he *lives*,"—having a clear view or the self-existence of the Lord Jesus Christ, the same yesterday, to-day, and for ever. And you and I looking back do not say, "I know that He *did live*, but He *lives* to-day." This very day you that mourn and sorrow for venerated friends, your

prop and pillar in years gone by, you may go to Christ with
confidence, because He not only lives, but He is the source of
life; and you therefore believe that He can give forth out of
Himself life to those whom you have committed to the tomb.
He is the Lord and giver of life originally, and He shall be
specially declared to be the resurrection and the life, when
the legions of His redeemed shall be glorified with Him. If I
saw no fountain from which life could stream to the dead, I
would yet believe the promise when God said that the dead
shall live; but when I see the fountain provided, and know
that it is full to the brim and that it runneth over, I can rejoice
without trembling. Since there is one who can say, "I am the
resurrection and the life," it is a blessed thing to see the means
already before us in the person of our Lord Jesus Christ. Let
us look up to our Goel then who liveth at this very time.

Still the marrow of Job's comfort it seems to me lay in that
little word "My." "I know that MY Redeemer liveth." Oh,
to get hold of Christ! I know that in His offices He is precious.
But, dear friends, we must get a property in Him before we can
really enjoy Him. What is honey in the wood to me, if like
the fainting Israelites, I dare not eat? It is honey in my hand,
honey on my lip, which enlightens mine eyes like those of Jonathan.
What is gold in the mine to me? Men are beggars in Peru, and
beg their bread in California. It is gold in my purse which
will satisfy my necessities, purchasing the bread I need. So,
what is a Kinsman if He be not a Kinsman to me. A Redeemer
that does not redeem me, an avenger who will never stand up
for my blood, of what avail were such? But Job's faith was
strong and firm in the conviction that the Redeemer was his.

Dear friends, dear friends, can all of you say, "I know that
my Redeemer liveth." The question is simple and simply put;
but oh, what solemn things hang upon your answer, "Is it MY
Redeemer?" I charge you rest not, be not content until by
faith you can say, "Yes, I cast myself upon Him; I am His,
and therefore He is mine." I know that full many of you, while
you look upon all else that you have as not being yours, yet can
say, "*My* Redeemer is mine." He is the only piece of property
which is really ours. We borrow all else, the house, the children;
nay, our very body we must return to the Great Lender. But
Jesus, we can never leave, for even when we are absent from
the body we are present with the Lord, and I know that even
death cannot separate us from Him, so that body and soul are
with Jesus truly even in the dark hours of death, in the long
night of the sepulchre, and in the separate state of spiritual
existence. Beloved, have you Christ? It may be you hold Him
with a feeble hand, you half think it is presumption to say,

"He is my Redeemer;" yet remember, if you have but faith as a grain of mustard seed, that little faith entitles you to say, and say now, "I know that my Redeemer liveth."

There is another word in this consoling sentence which no doubt served to give a zest to the comfort of Job. It was that he could say, "I KNOW"—"I KNOW that my Redeemer liveth." To say, "I hope so, I trust so," is comfortable; and there are thousands in the fold of Jesus who hardly ever get much further. But to reach the marrow of consolation you *must* say, "I KNOW." Ifs, buts, and perhapses, are sure murderers of peace and comfort. Doubts are dreary things in times of sorrow. Like wasps they sting the soul! If I have any suspicion that Christ is not mine, then there is vinegar mingled with the gall of death. But if I know that Jesus is mine, then darkness is not dark; even the night is light about me. Out of the lion cometh honey; out of the eater cometh forth sweetness. "I know that my Redeemer liveth." This is a brightly-burning lamp cheering the damps of the sepulchral vault, but a feeble hope is like a flickering smoking flax, just making darkness visible, but nothing more. I would not like to die with a mere hope mingled with suspicion. I might be safe with this but hardly happy; but oh, to go down into the river knowing that all is well, confident that as a guilty, weak, and helpless worm I have fallen into the arms of Jesus, and believing that He is able to keep that which I have committed to Him.

I would have you, dear Christian friends, never look upon the full assurance of faith as a thing impossible to you. Say not "It is too high; I cannot attain unto it." I have known one or two saints of God who have rarely doubted their interest at all. There are many of us who do not often enjoy any ravishing ecstacies, but on the other hand we generally maintain the even tenour of our way, simply hanging upon Christ, feeling that His promise is true, that His merits are sufficient, and that we are safe. Assurance is a jewel for worth but not for rarity. It is the common privilege of all the saints if they have but the grace to attain unto it, and this grace the Holy Spirit gives freely. Surely if Job in Arabia, in those dark misty ages when there was only the morning star and not the sun, when they saw but little, when life and immortality had not been brought to light,— if Job before the coming and advent still could say, "*I know*," you and I should not speak less positively. God forbid that our positiveness should be presumption.

Let us try ourselves, and see that our marks and evidences are right, lest we form an ungrounded hope; for nothing can be more destructive than to say, "Peace, peace, where there is no peace." But oh, let us build for eternity, and build solidly.

B

Let us not be satisfied with the mere foundation, for it is from the upper rooms that we get the widest prospect. Let us pray the Lord to help us to pile stone on stone, until we are able to say as we look at it, "Yes, I *know*, I KNOW that my Redeemer liveth." This, then, for present comfort to-day in the prospect of departure.

III. And now, in the third and last place, as THE ANTICIPATION OF FUTURE DELIGHT, let me call to your remembrance the other part of the text. Job not only knew that the Redeemer lived, but he anticipated the time when He should *stand in the latter day upon the earth.* No doubt Job referred here to our Saviour's first advent, to the time when Jesus Christ, "the goel," the Kinsman, should stand upon the earth to pay in the blood of His veins the ransom price, which had, indeed, in bond and stipulation been paid before the foundation of the world in promise. But I cannot think that Job's vision stayed there; he was looking forward to the second advent of Christ as being the period of the resurrection. We cannot endorse the theory that Job arose from the dead when our Lord died, although certain Jewish believers held this idea very firmly at one time. We are persuaded that "the latter day" refers to the advent of glory rather than to that of shame. Our hope is that the Lord shall come to reign in glory where He once died in agony.

The bright and hallowed doctrine of the second advent has been greatly revived in our churches in these latter days, and I look for the best results in consequence. There is always a danger lest it be perverted and turned by fanatical minds, by prophetic speculations, into an abuse; but the doctrine in itself is one of the most consoling, and, at the same time, one of the most practical, tending to keep the Christian awake, because the Bridegroom cometh at such an hour as we think not. Beloved, we believe that the same Jesus who ascended from Olivet shall so come in like manner as He ascended up into heaven. We believe in His personal advent and reign. We believe and expect that when both wise and foolish virgins shall slumber; in the night when sleep is heavy upon the saints; when men shall be eating and drinking as in the days of Noah, that suddenly as the lightning flasheth from heaven, so Christ shall descend with a shout, and the dead in Christ shall rise and reign with Him. We are looking forward to the literal, personal, and actual standing of Christ upon earth as the time when creation's groans shall be silenced for ever, and the earnest expectation of the creature shall be fulfilled.

Mark, that Job describes Christ as *standing.* Some interpreters have read the passage, "he shall stand in the latter days against the earth;" that as the earth has covered up the slain, as the earth has become the charnel-house of the dead, Jesus shall arise to the contest and say, "Earth, I am against thee; give up thy dead! Ye clods of the valley cease to be custodians of my people's bodies! Silent deeps, and you, ye caverns of the earth, deliver, once for all, those whom ye have imprisoned!" Macphelah shall give up its precious treasure, cemeteries and graveyards shall release their captives, and all the deep places of the earth shall resign the bodies of the faithful. Well, whether that be so or no, the posture of Christ, in standing upon the earth, is significant. It shows His triumph. He has triumphed over sin, which once like a serpent in its coils had bound the earth. He has defeated Satan. On the very spot where Satan gained his power Christ has gained the victory. Earth, which was a scene of defeated goodness, whence mercy once was all but driven, where virtue died, where everything heavenly and pure, like flowers blasted by pestilential winds, hung down their heads, withered and blighted—on this very earth everything that is glorious shall blow and blossom in perfection; and Christ Himself, once despised and rejected of men, fairest of all the sons of men, shall come in the midst of a crowd of courtiers, while kings and princes shall do Him homage, and all the nations shall call Him blessed. "He shall stand in the latter day upon the earth."

Then, at that auspicious hour, says Job, "In my flesh I shall see God." Oh, blessed anticipation—"I shall see God." He does not say, "I shall see the saints"—doubtless we shall see them all in heaven—but, "I shall see *God*." Note he does not say, "I shall see the pearly gates, I shall see the walls of jasper, I shall see the crowns of gold and the harps of harmony," but "I shall see God;" as if that were the sum and substance of heaven. "In my flesh shall I see *God*." The pure in heart shall see God. It was their delight to see Him in the ordinances by faith. They delighted to behold Him in communion and in prayer. There in heaven they shall have a vision of another sort. We shall see God in heaven, and be made completely like Him; the divine character shall be stamped upon us; and being made like to Him we shall be perfectly satisfied and content. Likeness to God, what can we wish for more? And a sight of God, what can we desire better? We shall see God, and so there shall be perfect contentment to the soul and a satisfaction of all the faculties.

Some read the passage, "Yet, I shall see God in my flesh," and hence think that there is here an allusion to Christ, our Lord Jesus Christ, as the word made flesh. Well, be it so, or be it not so, it is certain that we shall see Christ, and He, as the divine Redeemer, shall be the subject of our eternal vision. Nor shall we ever want any joy beyond simply that of seeing Him. Think not, dear friend, that this will be a narrow sphere for your mind to dwell in. It is but one source of delight, "I shall see God," but that source is infinite. His wisdom, His love, His power, all His attributes shall be subjects for your eternal contemplation, and as He is infinite under each aspect, there is no fear of exhaustion. His works, His purposes, His gifts, His love to you, and His glory in all His purposes, and in all His deeds of love—why, these shall make a theme that never can be exhausted. You may with divine delight anticipate the time when in your flesh you shall see God.

But I must have you observe how Job has expressly made us note that it is in the same body. "Yet, *in my flesh* shall I see God;" and then he says again, "whom I shall see for myself, and mine eye shall behold and not another." Yes, it is true that I, the very man standing here, though I must go down to die, yet I shall as the same man most certainly arise and shall behold my God. Not part of myself, though the soul alone shall have some view of God, but the whole of myself, my flesh, my soul, my body, my spirit shall gaze on God. We shall not enter heaven, dear friends, as a dismasted vessel is tugged into harbour; we shall not get to glory some on boards, and some on broken pieces of the ship, but the whole ship shall be floated safely into the haven, body and soul both being safe. Christ shall be able to say, "*All* that the father giveth to me shall come to me," not only all the persons, but all of the persons—each man in his perfection. There shall not be found in heaven one imperfect saint. There shall not be a saint without an eye, much less a saint without a body. No member of the body shall have perished; nor shall the body have lost any of its natural beauty. All the saints shall be all there, and all of all; the same persons precisely, only that they shall have risen from a state of grace to a state of glory. They shall be ripened; they shall be no more the green blades, but the full corn in the ear; no more buds but flowers; not babes but men.

Please to notice, and then I shall conclude, how the patriarch puts it as being a real personal enjoyment. "Whom mine eye shall behold, and not another." They shall not bring me a report as they did the Queen of Sheba, but I shall see Solomon the King for myself. I shall be able to say, as they did who spake to the woman of Samaria, "Now I believe, not because of thy word who did bring me a report, but I have seen him for myself." There shall be personal intercourse with God; not through the Book, which is but as a glass; not through the ordinances; but directly, in the person of our Lord Jesus Christ, we shall be able to commune with the Deity as a man talketh with his friend. "Not another." If I could be a changeling and could be altered, that would mar my comfort. Or if my heaven must be enjoyed by proxy, if draughts of bliss must be drunk for me, where were the hope? Oh, no; for myself, and not through another, shall I see God.

Have we not told you a hundred times that nothing but personal religion will do, and is not this another argument for it, because resurrection and glory are personal things? "Not another." If you could have sponsors to repent for you, then, depend upon it, you would have sponsors to be glorified for you. But as there is not another to see God for you, so you must yourself see and yourself find an interest in the Lord Jesus Christ.

In closing let me observe how foolish have you and I been when we have looked forward to death with shudders, with doubts, with loathings. After all, what is it? Worms! Do ye tremble at those base crawling things? Scattered particles! Shall we be alarmed at these? To meet the worms we have the angels; and to gather the scattered particles we have the voice of God. I am sure the gloom of death is altogether gone now that the lamp of resurrection burns. Disrobing is nothing now that better garments await us. We may long for evening to undress, that we may rise with God. I am sure my venerable friends now present, in coming so near as they do now to the time of the departure, must have some visions of the glory on the other side of the stream. Bunyan was not wrong, my dear brethren, when he put the land Beulah at the close of the pilgrimage. Is not my text a telescope which will enable you to see across the Jordan; may it not be as hands of angels to bring you bundles of myrrh and frankincense? You can say, "I know that my Redeemer liveth." You cannot want more; you were not satisfied with less in your youth, you will not be content with less now.

Those of us who are young, are comforted by the thought that we may soon depart. I say comforted, not alarmed by it; and we almost envy those whose race is nearly run, because we fear—and yet we must not speak thus, for the Lord's will be done—I was about to say, we fear that our battle may last long, and that mayhap our feet may slip; only He that keepeth Israel does not slumber nor sleep. So since we know that our Redeemer liveth, this shall be our comfort in life, that though we fall we shall not be utterly cast down; and since our Redeemer liveth, this shall be our comfort in death, that though worms destroy this body, yet in our flesh we shall see God.

May the Lord add His blessing on the feeble words of this morning, and to Him be glory for ever. Amen.

" Grave, the guardian of our dust!
   Grave, the treasury of the skies!
Every atom of thy trust
   Rests in hope again to rise.
Hark! the judgment trumpet calls;
   Soul, rebuild thy house of clay,
Immortality thy walls,
   And Eternity thy day."

RESURRECTION WITH CHRIST

A Sermon

Text.—"But God, who is rich in mercy, for his great love wherewith he loved us, even when we were dead in sins, hath quickened us together with Christ (by grace ye are saved)."—Ephesians ii. 4, 5.

THERE have been conferences of late of all sorts of people upon all kinds of subjects, but what a remarkable thing a conference would be if it were possible of persons who have been raised from the dead! If you could somehow or other get together the daughter of the Shunammite, the daughter of Jairus, the son of the widow at the gates of Nain, Lazarus, and Eutychus, what strange communings they might have one with another! what singular enquiries they might make, and what remarkable disclosures might they present to us! The thing is not possible, and yet a better and more remarkable assembly may be readily gathered on the same conditions, and more important information may be obtained from the confessions of its members.

This morning we have a conference of that very character gathered in this house; for many of us were dead in trespasses and sins, even as others, but we hope that through the divine energy we have been quickened from that spiritual death, and are now the living to praise God. It will be well for us to walk together, to review the past, to rejoice in the present, to look forward to the future. "You hath he quickened who were dead in trespasses and sins;" and as ye sit together, an assembly of men possessed of resurrection life, ye are a more notable conclave than if merely your bodies and not your spirits had been quickened.

The first part of this morning's discourse will be occupied with *a solemnity in which we shall take you into the charnel house ;* secondly, we shall spend a while in *reviewing a miracle*, and *we shall observe dead men living ;* we shall then turn aside to observe *a sympathy* indicated in the test; and we shall close with a song, for the text reads somewhat like music—it is full of thankfulness, and thankfulness is the essence of true song; it is full of holy and adoring wonder; it is evermore true poetry even though expressed in prose.

I. Celebrate first a great SOLEMNITY, and descend into the charnel house of our poor humanity.

According to the teaching of sacred Scripture, men are dead, spiritually dead. Certain vain men would make it out that men are only a little disordered and bruised by the fall, wounded in a few delicate members, but not mortally injured. However, the word of God is very express upon the matter, and declares our race to be not wounded, not hurt merely, but slain outright, and left as dead in trespasses and sin. There are those who fancy that fallen human nature is only in a sort of syncope or fainting fit, and only needs a process of reviving to set it right. You have only, by education and by other manipulations, to set its life-floods in motion, and to excite within it some degree of action, and then life will speedily be developed. There is much good in every man, they say, and you have only to bring it out by training and example.

This fiction is exactly opposite to the teaching of sacred Scripture. Within these truthful pages, we read of no fainting fit, no temporary paralysis, but death is the name for nature's condition, and quickening is its great necessity. Man is not partly dead, like the half-drowned mariner, in whom some spark of life may yet remain, if it be but fondly tendered, and wisely nurtured. There is not a spark of spiritual life left in man—manhood is to all spiritual things an absolute corpse. "In the day thou eatest thereof thou shalt surely die," said God to our first parents, and die they did—a spiritual death; and all their children alike by nature lie in this spiritual death, not a sham death, or a metaphorical one, but a real, absolute, spiritual death.

Yet it will be said, "Are they not alive?" Truly so, but not spiritually. There are grades of life. You come first upon the vegetable life; but the vegetable is a dead thing as to the vitality of the animal. Above the animal life rises the mental life, a vastly superior life; the creature, which is only an animal, is dead to either the joys or the sorrows of mental life. Then, high above the mental, as much as the mental is above the animal, rises what Scripture calls the spiritual life—the life in Christ Jesus. All men have more or less of the mental life, and it is well that they should cultivate it—get as much as they can of it, that they should put it to the best uses, and make it subserve the highest ends.

If you could conceive a man in all respects like yourselves, with this one difference, that his soul had died out of him, that he only possessed his animal faculties, but had no intellectual faculties, so that he could breathe and walk, sleep and eat, and drink, and make a noise, but all mental power was gone, you would then speak of him as being entirely dead to mental pursuits. He might be a most vigorous and well-developed animal, but his manhood would be dead. It would be of no use explaining a proposition to him, or working out a problem on the black board for his instruction, or offering him even the simplest school-book, for if he had no mind to receive, how could you impart?

Now, spiritually, this is the condition of every unregenerate man. It is of no use whatever, apart from the Spirit of God, to hope to make the man understand spiritual things, for they are spiritually discerned, says the apostle. The carnal mind cannot understand the things which be of God—when best trained it has no glimmering of the inward sense of spiritual things; it stumbles over the letter and loses the real meaning, not from want of mental capacity, but from the absence of spiritual life. O sons of men, if ye would know God, "Ye must be born again;" "Except a man be born again, he *cannot* see the kingdom of God," he cannot understand it, he cannot know it. The carnal man cannot understand the things which are of God, which are eternal and invisible, any more than an ox can understand astronomy, or a fish can admire the classics. Not in a moral sense, nor a mental sense, but in a spiritual sense, poor humanity is dead, and so the word of God again and again most positively describes it.

Step with me, then, into the sepulchre-house, and what do you observe of yonder bodies which are slumbering there? They are quite unconscious? Whatever goes on around them, neither occasions them joy nor causes them grief. The dead in their graves may be marched over by triumphant armies, but they shout not with them that triumph. Or, friends they have left behind may sit there, and water the grass upon the green mound with their tears, but no sigh responsive comes from the gloomy cavern of the tomb.

It is thus with men spiritually dead: they are unaffected by spiritual things. A dying Saviour, whose groans might move the very adamant, and make the rocks dissolve, they can hear of all unmoved. Even the all-present Spirit is undiscerned by them, and His power unrecognised. Angels, holy men, godly exercises, devout aspirations, all these are beyond and above their world. The pangs of hell do not alarm them, and the joys of heaven do not entice them. They hear after a sort mentally, but the spirit-ear is fast shut up, and they do not hear.

A man totally deaf is not startled by thunder-claps; if totally blind, he is not alarmed by the flashing of the lightning, he fears not the tempest which he does not discern. Even thus is it with you who are at ease in your sins, you cannot discern the danger of your sin, you do not perceive the terror that rises out of it, else let me tell you there were no sleep to those wanton

eyes, no rest to those giddy spirits; you would cry out in grief
the very moment you received life, nor would you rest till delivered
from those evils which now ensure for you a sure damnation.
Oh! were you but alive, you would never be quiet till you were
saved from the wrath to come. Man remains unconscious of
spiritual things and unmoved by them because, in a spiritual
sense, he is dead.

Invite yonder corpse to assist you in the most necessary works
of philanthropy. The pestilence is abroad, ask the buried one
to kneel with you and invoke the power of heaven to recall the
direful messenger; or, if he prefers it, ask him to assist you in
purifying the air and attending to sanitary arrangements. You
ask in vain, however needful or simple the act he cannot help
you in it. And in spiritual things, it is even so with the graceless.
The carnal man can put himself into the posture of prayer, but
he cannot pray; he can open his mouth and make sweet sounds
in earth-born music, but the true praise he is an utter stranger
to. Even repentance, that soft and gentle grace which ought to
be natural to the sinful, is quite beyond his reach. How shall
he repent of a sin the weight of which he cannot feel? How
shall he pray for a blessing the value of which he has no power
to perceive? How shall he praise a God in whom he feels no
interest, and in whose existence he takes no delight? I say that
to all spiritual things the man is quite as unable as the dead
are unable to the natural works and services of daily life.

"And yet," says one, "we heard you last Lord's-day tell these
dead people to repent and be converted." I know you did, and
you shall hear me yet again do the like. But why speak I to
the dead thus, and tell them to perform actions which they
cannot do? Because my Master bids me, and as I obey my Master's
errand, a power goes forth with the word spoken, and the dead
start in their sleep, and they wake through the quickening power
of the Holy Spirit, and they who naturally cannot repent and
believe, *do* repent and believe in Jesus, and escape from their
former sins and live; yet, believe me, it is no power of theirs
which makes them thus start from their death-sleep, and no
power of mine which arrests the guilty, slumbering conscience—
it is a power of divine which God has yoked with the word which
He has given forth when it is fully and faithfully preached.

Therefore have we exercised ourselves in our daily calling of
bidding dead men live, because life comes at the divine bidding.
But dead they are, most thoroughly so, and the longer we live
the more we feel it to be so; and the more closely we review
our own condition before conversion, and the more studiously
we look into our own condition even now, the more fully do
we know that man is dead in sin, and life is a gift, a gift from

heaven, a gift of undeserved love and sovereign grace, so that the living must every one of them praise God and not themselves.

One of the saddest reflections about poor dead human nature is what it will be. Death in itself, though a solemn matter, is not so dreadful as that which comes of it. Many a time when that dear corpse has first been forsaken of the soul, those who have lost a dear one have been fain to imprint that cold brow with kisses still. The countenance has looked even more lovely than in life, and when friends have taken the last glimpse, there has been nothing revolting, but much that was attractive. Our dead ones have smiled like sleeping angels, even when we were about to commit them to the grave. Ah! but we cannot shake from us a wretched sense of what is sure to be revealed before long. It is only a matter of time, and corruption must set in. So it is with us all. "When lust hath conceived, it bringeth forth sin: and sin, when it is finished, bringeth forth death;" and this, dear hearer, do we solemnly remind you will be your portion for ever and ever, unless God be pleased to quicken you. Unless you be made to live together with Christ you will be in this world dead, perhaps in this world corrupt, but certainly so in the next world, where all the dreadful influences of sin will be developed and discovered to the very full, and you shall be cast away from the presence of God and the glory of His power.

II. We now change the subject for something more pleasant, and observe A MIRACLE, or dead men made alive.

The great object of the gospel of Christ is to create men anew in Christ Jesus. It aims at resurrection, and accomplishes it. The gospel did not come into this world merely to restrain the passions or educate the principles of men, but to infuse into them a new life which, as fallen men, they did not possess. I saw yesterday what seemed to me a picture of those preachers whose sole end and aim is the moralising of their hearers, but who have not learned the need of supernatural life.

Not very far from the shore were a dozen or more boats at sea dragging for two dead bodies. They were using their lines and grappling irons, and what with hard rowing and industrious sailing, were doing their best most commendably to fish up the lost ones from the pitiless sea. I do not know if they were successful but if so, what further could they do with them but decently to commit them to their mother earth? The process of education and everything else, apart from the Holy Spirit, is a dragging for dead men, to lay them out decently, side by side, in the order and decency of death, but nothing more can man do for man.

The gospel of Jesus Christ has a far other and higher task: it does not deny the value of the moralist's efforts, or decry the results of education, but it asks what more can you do, and the response is, "Nothing." Then it bids the bearers of the bier stand away and make room for Jesus, at whose voice the dead arise. The preacher of the gospel cannot be satisfied with what is done in drawing men out of the sea of outward sin, he longs to see the lost life restored, he desires to have breathed into them a new and superior life to what they have possessed before. Go your way, education, do your best, you are useful in your sphere; go your way, teacher of morality, do your best, you too are useful in your own manner; but if it comes to what man really needs for eternity, you, all put together, are little worth —the gospel, and the gospel alone, answers to men's requirements: man must be regenerated, quickened, made anew, have fresh breath from heaven breathed into him, or the work of saving him is not begun. The text tells us that God has done this for His people, for those who trust in Him. Let us observe the dry bones as they stir and stand before the Lord, and observing, let us praise the Lord, that according to His great love wherewith He loved us, He hath quickened us together with Christ.

In this idea of quickening, there is a *mystery*. What is that invisible something which quickens a man? Who can unveil the secret? Who can track life to its hidden fountain? Brother, you are a living child of God: what made you live? You know that it was by the power of the Holy Spirit. In the language of the text, you trace it to God, you believe your new life to be of divine implantation. You are a believer in the supernatural; you believe that God has visited you as He has not visited other men, and has breathed into you life. You believe rightly, but you cannot explain it. We know not of the wind, whence it cometh or whither it goeth: so is every one that is born of the Spirit. He that should sit down deliberately and attempt to explain regeneration, and the source of it, might sit there till he grew into a marble statue before he would accomplish the task. The Holy Spirit enters into us, and we who were dead before to spiritual things, begin to live by His power and in-dwelling. He is the great worker, but how the Holy Spirit works is a secret that must be reserved for God Himself. We need not wish to understand the mode; it is enough for us if we partake of the result.

It is a great mystery then, but while it is a mystery it is a great *reality*. We know and do testify, and we have a right to be believed, for we trust we have not forfeited our characters, we know and do testify that we are now possessors of a life which we knew nothing of some years ago, that we have come to exist

in a new world, and that the appearance of all things outside
of us is totally changed from what it used to be. "Old things
have passed away, behold all things are become new." I bear
witness that I am this day the subject of sorrows which were
no sorrows to me before I knew the Lord, and that I am uplifted
with joys which I should have laughed at the very thought of
if any one had whispered the name of them in my ears before
the life divine had quickened me.

This is the witness of hundreds of us, and although others
disbelieve us, they have no right to deny our consciousness
because they have not partaken of the like. If they have never
tried it, what should they know about it? If there should be
an assembly of blind men, and one of them should have his
eyes opened, and begin to talk of what he saw, I can imagine
the blind ones all saying, "What a fool that man is! There
are no such things." "Here I have lived in this world seventy
years," says one, "and I never saw that thing which he calls
a colour, and I do not believe in his absurd nonsense about
scarlet and violet, and black and white; it is all foolery together."
Another wiseacre declares, "I have been up and down the
world, and all over it, for forty years, and I declare I never
had the remotest conception of blue or green, nor had my father
before me. He was a right good soul, and always stood up for
the grand old darkness. 'Give me,' said he, 'a good stick and
a sensible dog, and all your nonsensical notions about stars,
and suns, and moons, I leave to fools who like them.'" The
blind man has not come into the world of light and colour,
and the unregenerate man has not come into that world of
spirit, and hence neither of them is capable of judging correctly.

I sat one day, at a public dinner, opposite a gentleman of
the gourmand species, who seemed a man of vast erudition as
to wines and spirits, and all the viands of the table; he judged
and criticised at such a rate that I thought he ought to have
been employed by our provision merchants as taster in general.
He had finely developed lips, and he smacked them frequently.
His palate was in a fine critical condition. He was also as pro-
ficient in the quantity as in the quality, and disposed of meats
and drinks in a most wholesale manner. His retreating forehead,
empurpled nose, and protruding lips, made him, while eating
at least, more like an animal than a man. At last, hearing a
little conversation around him upon religious matters, he opened
his small eyes and his great mouth, and delivered himself of
this sage utterance, "I have lived sixty years in this world, and
I never felt or believed in anything spiritual in all my life."
The speech was a needless diversion of his energies from the
roast duck. We did not want him to tell us that. I, for one,

was quite clear about it before he spoke. If the cat under the table had suddenly jumped on a chair and said the same thing, I should have attached as much importance to the utterance of the one as to the declaration of the other; and so, by one sin in one man and another in another man, they betray their spiritual death. Until a man has received the divine life, his remarks thereon, even if he be an archbishop, go for nothing. He knows nothing about it according to his own testimony.

This life brings with it the *exercise of renewed faculties*. The man who begins to live unto God has powers now which he never had before: the power really to pray, the power heartily to praise, the power actually to commune with God, the power to see God, to talk with God, the power to receive tidings from the invisible world, and the power to send messages up through the veil which hides the unseen up to the very throne of God.

Suppose a man to have been dead, and to have been buried like others in some great necropolis, some city of the dead, in the catacombs. An angel visits him, and by mercy's touch he lives. Now, can you conceive that man's first emotion when he begins to breathe? There he is in the coffin—he feels stifled, pent up. He had been there twenty years, but he never felt inconvenienced until now. He was easy enough, in his narrow cell, if ease can be where life is not. The moment he lives he feels a horrible sense of suffocation, life will not endure to be so hideously compressed, and he begins to struggle for release. He lifts with all his might that dreadful coffin lid! What a relief when the decaying plank yields to his pressure!

So the ungodly man is content enough in his sin, his Sabbath-breaking, his covetousness, his worldliness, but the moment God quickens him his sin is as a sepulchre to the living, he feels unutterably wretched, he is not in a congenial position, and he struggles to escape. Often at the first effort the great black lid of blasphemy flies off, never to be replaced. Satan thought it was screwed down fast enough, and so it was for a dead man, but life makes short work of it, and many other iniquities follow. But to return to our resurrection in the vault: the man gasps a minute, and feels refreshed with such air as the catacomb affords him; but soon he has a sense of clammy damp about him, and feels faint and ready to expire. So the renewed man at first feels little but his inability, and groans after power, he cries, "I want to repent; I want to believe in Jesus; I want to be saved." Poor wretch! he never felt that before—of course he did not—he was dead; now he is alive, and hence he longs for the tokens, signs, fruits and refreshments of life.

That giddy ball-room—why, it was well enough for one who knew no better. That ale-bench was suitable for an unregenerate soul—but what can an heir of heaven do in such places? Lord, deliver me. Give me light and liberty. Bring my soul out of prison, that I may live and praise thy name. The man pines for liberty, and if, at last, he stumbles to the door of the vault and reaches the open air, methinks he drinks deep draughts of the blessed oxygen! How glad he is to look upon the green fields and the fresh flowers. You do not imagine that he will wish to return to the vaults again; he will utterly forsake those gloomy abodes; he shudders at the remembrance of the past, and would not for all the world undergo again what he has once passed through; he is tenderly affected at every remembrance of the past, and is especially fearful lest there should be others like himself newly quickened, who may need a brother's hand to set them at liberty; he loathes the place where once he slept so quietly.

So the converted man dreads the thought of going back to the joys which once so thoroughly fascinated him. "No," saith he, "they are no joys to me. They were joys well enough for my old state of existence, but now, having entered into a new life, a new world, they are no more joys to me than the spade and shroud are joys to a living man, and I can only think of them with grief, and of my deliverance with gratitude.

III. I must pass on very briefly to the third point. The text indicates A SYMPATHY: "He hath quickened us *together with Christ.*" What does that mean? It means that the life which lives in a saved man is the same life which dwells in Christ. To put it simply—when Elisha had been buried for some years, we read that they threw a man who was dead into the tomb where the bones of Elisha were, and no sooner did the corpse touch the prophet's bones than it lived at once. Yonder is the cross of Christ, and no sooner does the soul touch the crucified Saviour than it lives at once, for the Father hath given to Him to have life in Himself, and life to communicate to others. Whosoever trusts Christ has touched Him, and by touching Him he has received the virtue of eternal life: to trust in the Saviour of the world is be quickened through Him.

We are quickened together with Christ in three senses: First, *representatively.* Christ represents us before the eternal throne; He is the second Adam to His people. So long as the first Adam lived the race lived, and so long as the second Adam lives the race represented by Him lives before God. Christ is accepted, believers are accepted; Christ is justified, the saints are justified; Christ lives, and the saints enjoy a life which is hid with Christ in God.

Next we live by *union* with Christ. So long as the head is alive the members have life. Unless a member can be served from the head, and the body maimed, it must live so long as there is life in the head. So long as Jesus lives, every soul that is vitally united to Him, and is a member of His body, lives according to our Lord's own word, "Because I live ye shall live also." Poor Martha was much surprised that Christ should raise her brother from the dead, but He said, as if to surprise her still more, "Whosoever liveth and believeth in me shall never die. Believest thou this?" This is one of the things we are to believe, that when we have received the spiritual life, it is in union with the life of Christ, and consequently can never die; because Christ lives, our life must abide in us for ever.

Then we also live together with Christ as to *likeness*. We are quickened together with Christ, that is, in the same manner. Now, Christ's quickening was in this wise. He was dead through the law, but the law has no more dominion over Him now that He lives again. So you, Christian, you are cursed by the old law of Sinai, but it has no power to curse you now, for you are risen in Christ. You are not under the law; its terrors and threatenings have nought to do with you. Of our Lord it is written, "In that he liveth," it is said, "he liveth unto God." Christ's life is a life unto God. Such is yours. You are not henceforth to live unto the flesh to mind the things of it; but God who gave you life is to be the great object of your life; *in* Him you live, and *for* Him you live. Moreover, it is said, "Christ being raised from the dead dieth no more; death hath no more dominion over him." In that same way the Christian lives; he shall never go back to his spiritual death—having once received divine life, he shall never lose it. God plays not fast and loose with His chosen; He does not save to-day, and damn to-morrow. He does not quicken us with the inward life, and then leave us to perish; grace is a living, incorruptible seed, which liveth and abideth for ever. "The water that I shall give him," saith Jesus, "shall be in him a well of water springing up unto everlasting life." Glory be to God, then, you who live by faith in Christ live an immortal life, a life dedicated to God, a life of deliverance from the bondage of the law; rejoice in it, and give your God all the praise!

IV. And this brings us to the last word, which was A SONG. We have not time to sing it, we will just write the score before your eyes, and ask you to sing it at your leisure, your hearts making melody to God. Brethren and sisters, if you have indeed been thus made alive as others are not, you have first of all, in the language of the test, to praise *the great love* of God, great beyond all precedent. It was love which made Him breathe into Adam the breath of life, and make poor clay to walk and speak; but it is far greater love which makes Him now after the fall has defiled us, renew us with a second and yet higher life.

He might have made new creatures by millions out of nothing. He had but to speak, and angels would have thronged the air, or, beings like ourselves, only pure and unfallen, would have been multiplied by myriads upon the greensward. If He had left us to sink to hell as fallen angels had done before us, who could have impugned His justice? But His great love would not let Him leave His elect to perish. He loved His people, and therefore He would cause them to be born again, His great love wherewith He loved us, defied death, and hell, and sin. Dwell on the theme you who have partaken of this love! He loved *us*, the most unworthy, who had no right to such love: there was nothing in us to love, and yet He loved us, when we were dead. Here His great love seems to swell and rise to mountainous dimensions: love to miserable sinners, love to loathsome sinners, love to the dead and to the corrupt. Oh, heights and depths of sovereign grace, where are the notes which can sufficiently sound forth your praise? Sing, O ye redeemed, of His great love wherewith He loved us, even when we were dead in sins.

And cease not ye to praise God, as ye think of the riches of His mercy, for we are told that He is rich in mercy, rich in His nature as to mercy, rich in His covenant as to treasured mercy, rich in the person of His dear Son as to purchased mercy, rich in providential mercy, but richest of all in the mercy which saves the soul. Friends, explore the mines of Jehovah's wealth if you can. Take the key and open the granaries of your God and see the stores of love which He has laid up for you. Strike your sweetest notes to the praise of God, who is rich in mercy, for His great love wherewith He hath loved us.

And let the last note and the highest and the loudest of your song be that with which the text concludes, "By grace are ye saved." O never stammer there; brethren and sisters, whatever you do, hold or do not hold, never be slow to say this, "If saved at all, I am saved by grace; grace in contradistinction to human merit, for I have no merit; grace in contradistinction to my own free will, for my own free will would have led me further and further from God. Preventing grace brought me near to Him." Do bless and magnify the grace of God, and as you owe all to it cry, "Perish each thought of pride," consecrate yourself entirely to the God to whom you owe everything. Desire to help to spread the saviour of that grace which has brought such good things to you, and vow in the name of the quickening Spirit, that He who has made you live by faith shall, from this day till you enter into heaven, have the best of your thoughts, and

c

your words, and your actions, for you are not your own; you have been quickened from the dead, and you must live in newness of life.

The Lord bless you, dear friends; if you have never spiritually lived, may He give you grace to believe in Jesus this morning, and then you are alive from the dead; and if you are alive already, may He quicken you yet more and more by his eternal Spirit, till He brings you to the land of the living on the other side of the Jordan. Amen.

THE STONE ROLLED AWAY

A Sermon

Text.—"The angel of the Lord descended from heaven, and came and rolled back the stone from the door, and sat upon it."—Matthew xxviii. 2.

As the holy women went towards the sepulchre in the twilight of the morning, desirous to embalm the body of Jesus, they recollected that the huge stone at the door of the tomb would be a great impediment in their way, and they said one to another, "Who shall roll us away the stone?" That question gathers up the mournful enquiry of the whole universe. They seem to have put into language the great sigh of universal manhood, "Who shall roll us away the stone?" In man's path of happiness lies a huge rock, which completely blocks up the road. Who among the mighty shall remove the barrier? Philosophy attempted the task, but miserably failed. In the ascent to immortality the stone of doubt, uncertainty, and unbelief, stopped all progress. Who could upheave the awful mass, and bring life and immortality to light?

Men, generation after generation, buried their fellows; the all-devouring sepulchre swallowed its myriads. Who could stay the daily slaughter, or give a hope beyond the grave? There was a whisper of resurrection, but men could not believe in it. Some dreamed of a future state, and talked of it in mysterious poetry, as though it were all imagination and nothing more. In darkness and in twilight, with many fears and few guesses at the truth, men continued to enquire, "Who shall roll us away the stone?"

To the women there were three difficulties. The stone of itself was huge; it was stamped with the seal of the law; it was guarded by the representatives of power. To mankind there were the same three difficulties. Death itself was a huge stone not to be moved by any strength known to mortals: that death was evidently sent of God as a penalty for offences against His law—how could it therefore be averted, how removed? The red seal of God's vengeance was set upon that sepulchre's mouth—how should that seal be broken? Who could roll the stone away?

No answer was given to sages and kings, but the women who loved the Saviour found an answer. They came to the tomb of Christ, but it was empty, for Jesus had risen. Here is the answer to the world's enquiry—there is another life; bodies will live again, for Jesus lives. Sorrow no longer, ye mourners, around the grave, as those that are without hope; for since Jesus Christ is risen, the dead in Christ shall rise also. Wipe away those tears, for the believer's grave is no longer the place for lamentations, it is but the passage to immortality.

I purpose, this morning, to talk a little concerning the resurrection of our exalted Lord Jesus; and that the subject may the more readily interest you, I shall, first of all, *bid this stone which was rolled away, preach to you ;* and then shall invite you *to hear the angel's homily from his pulpit of stone.*

I. First, LET THE STONE PREACH.

It is not at all an uncommon thing to find in Scripture stones bidden to speak. Great stones have been rolled as witnesses against the people; stones and beams out of the wall have been called upon to testify to sin. I shall call this stone as a witness to valuable truths of which it was the symbol. The river of our thought divides into six streams.

1. First, the stone rolled must evidently be regarded as *the door of the sepulchre removed.* Death's house was firmly secured by a huge stone; the angel removed it, and the living Christ came forth. The massive door, you will observe, was taken away from the grave—not merely opened, but unhinged, flung aside, rolled away; and henceforth death's ancient prison-house is without a door. The saints shall pass in, but they shall not be shut in. They shall tarry there as in an open cavern, but there is nothing to prevent their coming forth from it in due time.

As Samson, when he slept in Gaza, and was beset by foes, arose early in the morning, and took up upon his shoulders the gates of Gaza—post, and bar, and all—and carried all away, and left the Philistine stronghold open and exposed, so has it been done unto the grave by our Master, Who, having slept out His three days and nights, according to the divine decree, arose in the greatness of His strength, and bore away the iron gates of the sepulchre, tearing every bar from its place. The removal of the imprisoning stone was the outward type of our Lord's having plucked up the gates of the grave—post, bar, and all— thus exposing that old fortress of death and hell, and leaving it as a city stormed and taken, and henceforth bereft of power.

Remember that our Lord was committed to the grave as a

hostage. "He died for our sins." Like a debt they were imputed to Him. He discharged the debt of obligation due from us to God, on the tree; He suffered to the full, the great substitutionary equivalent for our suffering, and then He was confined in the tomb as a hostage until His work should be fully accepted. That acceptance would be notified by His coming forth from durance vile; and that coming forth would become our justification—"He rose again for our justification." If He had not fully paid the debt He would have remained in the grave. If Jesus had not made effectual, total, final atonement, He must have continued a captive. But He had done it all. The "It is finished," which came from His own lips, was established by the verdict of Jehovah, and Jesus was set free.

Come, brethren, let us rejoice in this. In the empty tomb of Christ, we see sin for ever put away: we see, therefore, death most effectually destroyed. Our sins were the great stone which shut the mouth of the sepulchre, and held us captives in death, and darkness, and despair. Our sins are now for ever rolled away, and hence death is no longer a dungeon dark and drear, the ante-chamber of hell, but the rather it is a perfumed bed-chamber, a withdrawing room, the vestibule of heaven. For as surely as Jesus rose, so must His people leave the dead: there is nothing to prevent the resurrection of the saints. The stone which could keep us in the prison has been rolled away. Who can bar us in when the door itself is gone? Who can confine us when every barricade is taken away?

> "Who shall rebuild for the tyrant his prison?
> The sceptre lies broken that fell from his hands;
> The stone is removed; the Lord is arisen:
> The helpless shall soon be released from their bands."

2. In the second place, regard the stone as *a trophy set up*.

As men of old set up memorial stones, and as at this day we erect columns to tell of great deeds of prowess, so that stone rolled away was, as it were, before the eyes of our faith consecrated that day as a memorial of Christ's eternal victory over the powers of death and hell. They thought that they had vanquished Him; they deemed that the Crucified was overcome. Grimly did they smile as they saw His motionless body wrapped in the winding-sheet and put away in Joseph's new tomb; but their joy was fleeting; their boastings were but brief, for at the appointed moment He who could not see corruption rose and came forth from beneath their power. His heel was bruised by the old serpent, but on the resurrection morning He crushed the dragon's head.

" Vain the stone, the watch, the seal,
  Christ has burst the gates of hell;
Death in vain forbids His rise,
  Christ hath open'd Paradise.

Lives again our glorious King!
  ' Where, O death, is now thy sting?'
Once He died our souls to save;
  ' Where's thy victory, boasting grave?'"

Brethren beloved in Christ, as we look at yonder stone, with the angel seated upon it, it rises before us as a monument of Christ's victory over death and hell, and it becomes us to remember that His victory was achieved for us, and the fruits of it are all ours. We have to fight with sin, but Christ has overcome it. We are tempted by Satan: Christ has given Satan a defeat. We by-and-by shall leave this body; unless the Lord come speedily, we may expect to gather up our feet like our fathers, and go to meet our God; but death is vanquished for us, and we can have no cause to fear. Courage, Christian soldiers, you are encountering a vanquished enemy: remember that the Lord's victory is a guarantee for yours. If the Head conquers, the members shall not be defeated. Let not sorrow dim your eye; let no fears trouble your spirit; you must conquer, for Christ has conquered. Awaken all your powers to the conflict, and nerve them with the hope of victory. Set up that stone before your faith's eye this morning, and say, "Here my Master conquered hell and death, and in His name and by His strength I shall be crowned, too, when the last enemy is destroyed."

3. For a third use of this stone, observe that here is *a foundation laid.* That stone rolled away from the sepulchre, typifying and certifying as it does the resurrection of Jesus Christ, is a foundation-stone for Christian faith. The fact of the resurrection is the key-stone of Christianity. Disprove the resurrection of our Lord, and our holy faith would be a mere fable; there would be nothing for faith to rest upon if He who died upon the tree did not also rise again from the tomb; then "your faith is vain;" said the apostle, "ye are yet in your sins," while "they also which are fallen asleep in Christ are perished." All the great doctrines of our divine religion fall asunder like the stones of an arch when the key-stone is dislodged, in a common ruin they are all overthrown, for all our hope hinges upon that great fact. If Jesus rose, then is this gospel what it professes to be; if He rose not from the dead, then is it all deceit and delusion.

But, brethren, that Jesus rose from the dead is a fact better established than almost any other in history. The witnesses were many: they were men of all classes and conditions. None of them ever confessed himself mistaken or deceptive. They were so persuaded that it was the fact, that the most of them suffered death for bearing witness to it. They had nothing to gain by such a witnessing; they did not rise in power, nor gain honour or wealth; they were truthful, simple-minded men who testified what they had seen and bore witness to that which they had beheld.

The resurrection is a fact better attested than any event recorded in any history whether ancient or modern. Here is the confidence of the saints; our Lord Jesus Christ, who witnessed a good confession before Pontius Pilate, and was crucified, dead, and buried, rose again from the dead, and after forty days ascended to the throne of God. We rest in Him; we believe in Him. If He had not risen, we had been of all men most miserable to have been His followers. If He had not risen, His atonement would not have been proved sufficient. If He had not risen, His blood would not have been to us proven to be efficacious for the taking away of sin; but as He has risen, we build upon this truth; all our confidence we rest upon it, and we are persuaded that—

> " Raised from the dead, He goes before;
> He opens heaven's eternal door;
> To give His saints a blest abode,
> Near their Redeemer and their God."

My dear hearers, are you resting your everlasting hopes upon the resurrection of Jesus Christ from the dead? Do you trust in Him, believing that He both died and rose again for you? Do you place your entire dependence upon the merit of His blood certified by the fact of His rising again?

If so, you have a foundation of fact and truth, a foundation against which the gates of hell shall not prevail; but if you are building upon anything that you have done, or anything that priestly hands can do for you, you are building upon the sands which shall be swept away by the all-devouring flood, and you and your hopes too shall go down into the fathomless abyss wrapped in the darkness of despair. Oh, to build upon the living stone of Christ Jesus! Oh, to rest on Him who is a tried corner-stone, elect, precious! This is to build safely, eternally, and blessedly.

4. A fourth voice from the stone is this: here is *rest provided*. The angel seemed to teach us that as he sat down upon the stone. How leisurely the whole resurrection was effected! How noiselessly, too! What an absence of pomp and parade! The angel descended, the stone was rolled away, Christ rose, and then the angel sat down on the stone. He sat there silently

and gracefully, breathing defiance to the Jews and to their seal, to the Roman legionaries and their spears, to death, to earth, to hell. He did as good as say, "Come and roll that stone back again, ye enemies of the risen One. All ye infernal powers, who thought to prevail against our ever-living Prince, roll back that stone again, if so ye dare or can!" The angel said not this in words, but his stately and quiet sitting upon the stone meant all that and more. The Master's work is done, and done for ever, and this stone, no more to be used, this unhinged door, no more employed to shut in the charnel house, is the type that "it is finished"—finished so as never to be undone, finished so as to last eternally. Yon resting angel softly whispers to us, "Come hither, and rest also." There is no fuller, better, surer, safer rest for the soul than in the fact that the Saviour in whom we trust has risen from the dead.

Do you mourn departed friends to-day? O come and sit upon this stone, which tells you they shall rise again. Do you soon expect to die? Is the worm at the root? Have you the flush of consumption on your cheek? O come and sit you down upon this stone, and bethink you that death has lost its terror now, for Jesus has risen from the tomb. Come you, too, ye feeble and trembling ones, and breathe defiance to death and hell. The angel will vacate his seat for you, and let you sit down in the face of the enemy. Though you be but a humble woman, or a man broken down, and wan, and languid with long years of weary sickness, yet may you well defy the hosts of hell, while resting down upon this precious truth, "He is not here, but He is risen: He has left the dead, no more to die."

> " Every note with wonders swell,
>   Sin o'erthrown, and captived hell;
>   Where is hell's once dreaded king?
>   Where, O death, thy mortal sting?
>   Hallelujah."

5. In the fifth place, that stone was *a boundary appointed*. Do you not see it so? Behold it then, there it lies, and the angel sits upon it. On that side see what you? The guards affrighted, stiffened with fear, like dead men. On this side what see you? The timid trembling women, to whom the angel softly speaks, "Fear not ye: for I know that ye seek Jesus." You see, then, that stone became the boundary between the living and the dead, between the seekers and the haters, between the friends and the foes of Christ. To His enemies His resurrection is "a stone of stumbling, and a rock of offence;" as of old on Mar's Hill, when the sages heard of the resurrection, they mocked.

But to His own people, the resurrection is the head-stone of the corner. Our Lord's resurrection is our triumph and delight.

The resurrection acts much in the same manner as the pillar which Jehovah placed between Israel and Egypt: it was darkness to Egypt, but it gave light to Israel. All was dark amidst Egypt's hosts, but all was brightness and comfort amongst Israel's tribes. So the resurrection is a doctrine full of horror to those who know not Christ, and trust Him not. What have they to gain by resurrection? Oh, the horrors of that tremendous morning, when every sinner shall rise, and the risen Saviour shall come in the clouds of heaven, and all the holy angels with Him! Truly there is nothing but dismay for those who are on the evil side of that resurrection stone.

But how great the joy which the resurrection brings to those who are on the right side of that stone! How they look for His appearing with daily growing transport! How they build upon the sweet truth that they shall arise, and with these eyes their Saviour see! I would have you ask yourselves, this morning, on which side you are of that boundary stone now. Have you life in Christ? Are you risen with Christ? Do you trust alone in Him who rose from the dead? If so, fear not ye: the angel comforts you, and Jesus cheers you; but oh! if you have no life in Christ, but are dead while you live, let the very thought that Jesus is risen, strike you with fear, and make you tremble, for tremble well you may, at that which awaits you.

6. Sixthly, I conceive that this stone may be used, and properly too, as *foreshadowing ruin*. Our Lord came into this world to destroy all the works of the devil. Behold before you the works of the devil pictured as a grim and horrible castle, massive and terrible, overgrown with the moss of ages, colossal, stupendous, cemented with blood of men, ramparted by mischief and craft, surrounded with deep trenches, and garrisoned with fiends. A structure dread enough to cause despair to every one who goeth round about it to count its towers and mark its bulwarks. In the fulness of time our Champion came into the world to destroy the works of the devil. During His life He sounded an alarm at the great castle, and dislodged here and there a stone, for the sick were healed, the dead were raised, and the poor had the gospel preached unto them. But on the resurrection morning the huge fortress trembled from top to bottom; huge rifts were in its walls; and tottering were all its strongholds. A stronger than the master of that citadel had evidently entered it and was beginning to overturn, overturn, overturn, from pinnacle to basement. One huge stone, upon which the building much depended, a corner-stone which knit the whole fabric together, was lifted bodily from its bed and hurled to the ground.

Jesus tore the huge granite stone of death from its position, and so gave a sure token that every other would follow. When that stone was rolled away from Jesus' sepulchre, it was a prophecy that every stone of Satan's building should come down, and not one should rest upon another of all that the powers of darkness had ever piled up, from the days of their first apostacy even unto the end.

Brethren, that stone rolled away from the door of the sepulchre gives me glorious hope. Evil is still mighty, but evil will come down. Spiritual wickedness reigns in high places; the multitude still clamour after evil; the nations still sit in thick darkness; many worship the scarlet woman of Babylon, others bow before the crescent of Mohammed, and millions bend themselves before blocks of wood and stone; the dark places and habitations of the earth are full of cruelty still; but Christ has given such a shiver to the whole fabric of evil that, depend upon it, every stone will be certain to fall. We have but to work on, use the battering-ram of the gospel, continue each one to keep in his place, and like the hosts around Jericho, to sound the trumpet still, and the day must come when every hoary evil, every colossal superstition, shall be laid low, even with the ground, and the prophecy shall be fulfilled, "Overturn, overturn, overturn it; and it shall be no more, until he come whose right it is; and I will give it him." That loosened stone on which the angel sits is the sure prognostic of the coming doom of everything that is base and vile. Rejoice, ye sons of God, for Babylon's fall draweth near. Sing, O heavens, and rejoice, O earth, for there shall not an evil be spared. Verily, I say unto you, there shall not be one stone left upon another, which shall not be cast down.

Thus has the stone preached to us; we will pause awhile and hear what the angel has to say.

II. THE ANGEL PREACHED two ways: he preached in symbol, and he preached in words.

Preaching *in symbol* is very popular with a certain party nowadays. The gospel is to be seen by the eye, they tell us, and the people are to learn from the change of colours, at various seasons, such as blue, and green, and violet, exhibited on the priest and the altar, and by lace and by candles, and by banners, and by cruets, and shells full of water; they are even to be taught or led by the nose, which is to be indulged with smoke of incense; and drawn by the ears, which are to listen to hideous intonings or to dainty canticles. Now, mark well that the angel was a symbolical preacher, with his brow of lightning and his robe of snow; but you will please to notice for whom the symbols were reserved. He did not say a word to the keepers—not a word. He gave them the symbolical gospel, that is to say, he looked upon them—and his glance was lightning; he revealed himself to them in his snow-white garments, and no more. Mark how they quake and tremble! That is the gospel of symbols; and wherever it comes it condemns. It can do no other. Why, the old Mosaic law of symbols, where did it end? How few ever reached its inner meaning! The mass of Israel fell into idolatry, and the symbolic system became death to them. The gospel message is, "Hear, and your soul shall live"; "Incline your ear, and come unto me." This is the life-giving message, "Believe in the Lord Jesus Christ, and thou shalt be saved." But, O perverse generation, if ye look for symbols and signs, ye shall be deluded with the devil's gospel, and fall a prey to the destroyer.

Now we will listen to the angel's sermon *in words*. Thus only is a true gospel to be delivered. Christ is the Word, and the gospel is a gospel of words and thoughts. It does not appeal to the eye; it appeals to the ear, and to the intellect, and to the heart. It is a spiritual thing, and can only be learned by those whose spirits are awakened to grasp at spiritual truth. The first thing the angel said was, "Fear not ye." Oh! this is the very genius of our risen Saviour's gospel—"Fear not ye." Ye who would be saved, ye who would follow Christ, ye need not fear. Did the earth quake? Fear not ye: God can preserve you though the earth be burned with fire. Did the angel descend in terrors? Fear not ye: there are no terrors in heaven for the child of God who comes to Jesus' cross, and trusts his soul to Him who bled thereon. Poor women, is it the dark that alarms you? Fear not ye: God sees and loves you in the dark, and there is nothing in the dark or in the light beyond His control.

Are you afraid to come to a tomb? Does a sepulchre alarm you? Fear not ye: you cannot die. Since Christ has risen, though you were dead yet should you live. Oh, the comfort of the gospel! Permit me to say there is nothing in the Bible to make any man fear who puts his trust in Jesus. Nothing in the Bible, did I say? There is nothing in heaven, nothing on earth, nothing in hell, that need make you fear who trust in Jesus. "Fear not ye." The past you need not fear, it is forgiven you; the present you need not fear, it is provided for; the future also is secured by the living power of Jesus. "Because I live," saith He, "ye shall live also." Fear! Why that were comely and seemly when Christ was dead, but now that He lives there remains no space for it? Do you fear your sins? They are all gone, for Christ had not risen if He had not put them all away. What is it you fear? If an angel bids you "Fear not," why will you fear? If every wound of the risen Saviour, and every act of your reigning Lord consoles you, why are you still dismayed? To be doubting, and fearing, and trembling, now that Jesus has risen, is an inconsistent thing in any believer. Jesus is able to succour you in all your temptations; seeing He ever liveth to make intercession for you, He is able to save you to the uttermost: therefore, do not fear.

Notice the next words, "Fear not ye: for I know." What! does an angel know the women's hearts? Did the angel know what Magdalene was about! Do spirits read our spirits? 'Tis well. But oh! 'tis better to remember that our heavenly Father knows. Fear not ye, for God knows what is in your heart. You have never made an avowal of anxiety about your soul, you are too bashful even for that; you have not even proceeded so far as to dare to say that you hope you love Jesus; but God knows your desires. Poor heart, you feel as if you could not trust, and could not do anything that is good; but you do at least desire, you do at least seek. All this God knows; with pleasure he spies out your desires. "Fear not ye," for your heavenly Father knows. Lie still, poor patient, for the surgeon knows where the wound is, and what it is that ails thee. Hush, my child, be still upon thy great Parent's bosom, for He knows all; and ought not that content thee, for His care is as infinite as His knowledge?

Then the angel went on to say, "Fear not ye: for I know that ye seek Jesus, which was crucified." There was room for comfort here. They were seeking Jesus, though the world had crucified Him. Though the many had turned aside and left Him, they were clinging to Him in loving loyalty. Now, is there any one here who can say, "Though I am unworthy to be a follower of Christ, and often think that He will reject me, yet there is one thing I am sure of—I would not be afraid of the fear of man for His sake. My sins make me fear, but no man could do it. I would stand at His side if all the world were against Him. I would count it my highest honour that the crucified One of the world should be the adored One of my heart. Let all the world cast Him out, if He would but take me in, poor unworthy worm as I am, I would never be ashamed to own His blessed and gracious Name." Ah! then, do not fear, for if that is how you feel towards Christ, He will own you in the last great day. If you are willing to own Him now, "Fear not ye."

Then he adds, "He is not here, for he is risen." Here is the instruction which the angel gives. After giving comfort, he gives instruction. Your great ground and reason for consolation, seeker, is that you do not seek a dead Christ, and you do not pray to a buried Saviour; He is really alive. To-day He is as able to relieve you, if you go to your closet and pray to Him, as He was to help the poor blind man when He was on earth. He is as willing to-day to accept and bless you as He was to bless the leper, or to heal the paralytic. Go to Him then at once, poor seeker; go to Him with holy confidence, for He is not here, He would be dead if He were—He is risen, living, and reigning, to answer your request.

The angel bade the holy women investigate the empty tomb, but, almost immediately after, he gave them a commission to perform on their Lord's behalf. Now, if any seeker here has been comforted by the thought that Christ lives to save, let him do as the angel said, let him go and tell to others of the good news that he has heard. O you who have learned of Jesus, keep not the blessed secret to yourselves. To-day, in some way or other, I pray you make known that Jesus Christ is risen. Pass the watchword round, as the ancient Christians did. On the first day of the week they said to one another, "The Lord is risen indeed."

If any ask you what you mean by it, you will then be able to tell them the whole of the gospel, for this is the essence of the gospel, that Jesus Christ died for our sins, and rose again the third day, according to the Scriptures—died the substitute for us criminals, rose the representative of us pardoned sinners— died that our sins might die, and lives again that our souls may live. Diligently invite others to come and trust Jesus. Tell them that there is life for the dead in a look at Jesus crucified; tell them that that look is a matter of the soul, it is a simple confidence; tell them that none ever did confide in Christ and were cast away; tell them what you have felt as the result of your trusting Jesus, and who can tell, many disciples will be added to His church, a risen Saviour will be glorified, and you will be comforted by what you have seen! The Lord follow these feeble words with His own blessing, for Christ's sake. Amen.

THE COMING RESURRECTION

A Sermon

Text.—"Marvel not at this: for the hour is coming, in the which all that are in the graves shall hear his voice, and shall come forth; they that have done good, unto the resurrection of life; and they that have done evil, unto the resurrection of damnation."—John v. 28, 29.

The doctrine of the resurrection of the dead is peculiarly a Christian belief. With natural reason, assisted by some little light lingering in tradition, or borrowed from the Jews, a few philosophers spelled out the immortality of the soul; but that the body should rise again, that there should be another life for this corporeal frame, was a hope which is brought to light by the revelation of Christ Jesus. Men could not have imagined so great a wonder, and they prove their powerlessness to have invented it, by the fact, that still, as at Athens, when they hear of it for the first time, they fall to mocking. "Can these dry bones live?" is still the unbeliever's sneer.

The doctrine of the resurrection is a lamp kindled by the hand which once was pierced. It is indeed in some respects the keystone of the Christian arch. It is linked in our holy faith with the person of Jesus Christ, and is one of the brightest gems in His crown. What if I call it the signet on His finger, the seal by which He hath proven to a demonstration, that He hath the king's authority, and hath come forth from God? The doctrine of resurrection ought to be preached much more commonly than it is as vital to the gospel. Listen to the apostle Paul as he describes the gospel which he preached, and by which true believers were saved: "I delivered unto you," saith he, "first of all that which I received, how that Christ died for our sins according to the Scriptures; and that he was buried, and that he rose again the third day according to the Scriptures."

From the resurrection of Christ, he argues that of all the dead, and insists upon it, that if Christ be not risen, both their faith and his preaching were vain. The doctrine of the resurrection in the early church was the main battle-axe and weapon of war of the preacher. Wherever the first missionaries went they made this prominent, that there would be a judgment, and that the dead should rise again to be judged by the Man Christ Jesus, according to their gospel. If we would honour Christ Jesus the Risen One, we must give prominence to this truth.

Moreover, the doctrine is continually blessed of God to arouse the minds of men. When we fancy that our actions are confined to this present life, we are careless of them, but when we discover that they are far-reaching, and that they cast influences for good or evil athwart an eternal destiny, then we regard them more seriously. What trumpet call can be more startling, what arousing voice can be more awakening than this news to the careless sinner that there is a life hereafter, that men must stand before the judgment-seat of Christ to receive for the things done in their bodies whether they be good or evil? Such doctrine I shall try to preach this morning for just such ends, for the honouring of Christ, for the awakening of the careless. God send us good speed and abundance of the desired results.

We shall first *expound the text*, and then secondly, *endeavour to learn its lessons*.

I. First we shall EXPOUND THE TEXT. No exposition will be more instructive than a verbal one. We will take each word and weigh its meaning.

Observe then, first, in the text there is a forbidding to marvel. "*Marvel not at this.*" Our Saviour had been speaking of two forms of life-giving which belonged to Himself as the Son of Man. The first was the power to raise the dead from their graves to a renewed natural life. He proved this on one or two occasions in His lifetime, at the gates of Nain, in the chamber of the daughter of Jairus, and again at the tomb of the almost rotting Lazarus. Jesus had power when He was on earth and has power still, if so He should will it, to speak to those who have departed, and bid them return again to this mortal state and reassume the joys and sorrows and duties of life. "As the Father raiseth up the dead, and quickeneth them; even so the Son quickeneth whom he will."

After our Lord had dwelt for a moment upon that form of His life-giving prerogative, He passed on to a second display of it, and testified that the time was then present when His voice was heard to the quickening of the spiritually dead. The spiritually dead—the men who are dead to holiness and dead to faith, dead to God and dead to grace; the men that lie enshrouded in the grave clothes of evil habits, rotting in the coffins of their depravity, deep down in the graves of their transgressions—these men, when Jesus speaks in the gospel, are made to live; a spiritual life is given to them, their dead souls are raised out of their long and horrible sleep, and they are en-livened with the life of God.

Now, both of these forms of quickening are worthy to be marvelled at. The resurrection of the natural man to natural life is a great wonder; who would not go a thousand miles to see such a thing performed? The raising up of the dead spirit to spiritual life, this is a greater wonder by far.

To you, dear brethren in the faith, the quickening of the dead is not so great a marvel as the saving of dead souls; and, indeed, the raising of a corpse from the grave is by no means so great a marvel as the raising up of a dead soul from the sleep of sin. For in the raising up of a dead body there is no opposition to the fiat of Omnipotence. God speaketh, and it is done; but in the saving of a dead soul, the elements of death within are potent, and these resist the life-giving power of grace, so that regeneration is a victory as well as a creation, a complicated miracle, a glorious display both of grace and power.

Beloved, let us humbly learn one lesson from this. We are ourselves by nature very like the Jews; we wonder mistrustfully, we unbelievingly wonder when we see or hear of fresh displays of the greatness of our Lord Jesus Christ. So narrow are our hearts, that we cannot receive His glory in its fulness. Ah, we love Him, and we trust Him, and we believe Him to be the fairest, and the greatest, and the best, and the mightiest, but if we had a fuller view of what He can do, the probabilities are that our amazement would be mingled with no small portion of doubt. As yet we have but slender ideas of our Lord's glory and power. We hold the doctrine of His deity, we are orthodox enough, but we have not thoroughly realised the fact that He is Lord God Almighty. Does not it sometimes seem to you to be impossible that such-and-such a grievously ungodly man could be converted? But why impossible with Him who can raise the dead? Does it not seem impossible that you could ever be supported through your present trouble? But how impossible with Him who shall make the dry bones live, and cause the sepulchre to disgorge? It appears improbable at times that your corruptions should ever be cleansed away, and that you should be perfect and without spot. But why so? He who is able to present tens of thousands of bodies before His throne, who long have slept in the sepulchre, and mouldered into dust, what can He not accomplish within His people?

O doubt no more, and let not even the greatest wonders of His love, His grace, His power, or His glory, cause you to marvel unbelievingly, but rather say as each new prodigy of His divine power rises before you, "I expected this of such a one as He is. I gathered that He could achieve this, for I understood that He was able to subdue all things to Himself. I knew that He fashioned the worlds, and built the heavens, and guided the stars, and that by Him all things consist, I am not therefore astounded though I behold the greatest marvels of His power." The first words of the text, then, urge us to faith, and rebuke all unbelieving amazement.

To the second sentence I now call your attention. The coming hour. "*The hour cometh,*" saith Christ. I suppose He calls it an hour, to intimate how very near it is in His esteem, since we do not begin to look at the exact hour of an event when it is extremely remote. An event which will not occur for hundreds of years is at first looked for and noted by the year, and only when we are reasonably near it do men talk of the day of the month, and we are coming very near it when we look for the precise hour. Christ intimates to us, that whether we think so or not, in God's thought the day of resurrection is very near; and though it may be a thousand years off even now, yet still to God it is but one day, and He would have us endeavour to think God's thought about it, not reckon any time to be long, since if it be time at all it must be short, and will be so regarded by us when it is past, and the day has arrived. This is practical wisdom, to bring close up to us that which is inevitable, and to act towards it as though it were but to-morrow morning when the trump should sound, and we should be judged.

"The hour is coming," saith the Saviour. He here teaches us the certainty of that judgment. The hour cometh; it assuredly cometh. In the divine decree this is the day for which all other days were made; and if it were possible that any determination of the Almighty could be changed, yet this never shall be, for "he hath appointed a day, in the which he will judge the world in righteousness by that man whom he hath ordained; whereof he hath given assurance unto all men, in that he hath raised him from the dead." "The hour cometh." Reflect, my brethren, that most solemn hour cometh every moment. Every second brings it nearer. While you have been sitting still in this house, you have been borne onwards towards that great event. As the pendulum of yonder clock continues unceasingly to beat like the heart of time, as morning dawn gives place to evening shade, and the seasons follow in constant cycle, we are drifted along the river of time nearer to the ocean of eternity. Borne as on the wings of some mighty angel who never pauses in his matchless flight, I onward journey towards the judgment bar of God. My brethren, by that selfsame flight are you also hurried on. Look to the resurrection, then, as a thing that ever cometh, silently drawing nearer and nearer hour by hour. Such contemplations will be of the utmost service to you.

D

Our Lord's words read as if the one hour of which He spake completely drove into the shade all other events; as if the hour, the one hour, the last hour, THE hour *par excellence*, the master hour, the royal hour, was of all hours the only hour that was coming that was worth mentioning as being inevitable and important. Like Aaron's rod, the judgment hour swallows up every other hour. We hear of hours that have been big with the fate of nations, hours in which the welfare of millions trembled in the balances, hours in which for peace or war the die must be cast, hours that have been called crises of history; and we are apt to think that frequently periods such as this occur in the world's history: but here is the culminating crisis of all, here is the iron hour of severity, the golden hour of truth, the clear sapphire hour of manifestations.

In that august hour there shall be proclamation made of the impartial decisions of the Lord Christ with regard to all the souls and bodies of men. Oh, what an hour is this which cometh on apace! My dear brethren, now and then I covet the tongue of the eloquent, and now I do so that I might on such a theme as this fire your imaginations and inflame your hearts; but let me pray you assist me now for a moment, and since this hour cometh, try to think it very very near. Suppose it should come *now* while we are here assembled; suppose that even now the dead should rise, that in an instant this assembly should be melted into the infinitely greater one, and that no eye should be fixed upon the forgotten preacher, but all fixed upon the great descending Judge, sitting in majesty upon His great white throne, I pray you bethink yourselves as though the curtain were uplifted, at this moment; anticipate the sentence which will come forth to you from the throne of righteousness, consider as though at this precise moment it were pronounced upon you! Oh now, pray you examine yourselves as though the testing days were come, for such an examination will be to your souls' benefit if you be saved, and they may be to your souls' arousing if you be unconverted.

But we must pass on. "Marvel not at this: the hour is coming when all that are in the graves." Notice this very carefully, "*all that are in the graves*," by which term is meant, not only all whose bodies are actually in the grave at this time, but all who ever were buried even though they may have been disinterred, and their bones may have mingled with the elements, been scattered by the winds, dissolved in the waves, or merged into vegetable forms. All who have lived and died shall certainly rise again. All! Compute then the numberless number! Count ye now the countless! How many lived before the deluge? It has been believed, and I think accurately, that the inhabitants of this world, were more numerous at the time of the deluge than they probably are now, owing to the enormous length of human life; men's numbers were not so terribly thinned by death as they are now.

Think if you will from the times of the deluge onward, of all Adam's progeny. From Tarshish to Sinim men covered the lands. Nineveh, Babylon, Chaldea, Persia, Greece, Rome, these were vast empires of men. The Parthians, Scythians, and Tartar hordes, who shall reckon up? As for those northern swarms of Goths and Huns and Vandals, these were continually streaming as from a teeming hive, in the middle ages, and Frank and Saxon and Celt multiplied in their measure. Yet these nations were but types of a numerous band of nations even more multitudinous. Think of Ethiopia and the whole continent of Africa; remember India and Japan, and the land of the setting sun; in all lands great tribes of men have come and have gone to rest in their sepulchres. What millions upon millions must lie buried in China and Burmah! What innumerable hosts are slumbering in the land of the pyramids and the mummy pits! Every one, both great and small, embalmed of old in Egypt, who shall compute the number?

Hear ye then and believe—out of all who have ever lived of woman born, not one shall be left in the tomb; all, all shall rise. I may well say as the psalmist did of another matter, "Such knowledge is too wonderful for me; it is high, I cannot attain unto it." How hath God marked all these bodies, how hath He tracked the form of each corporeal frame? How shall Jesus Christ be able to raise all these? I know not, but He shall do it, for so He declareth and so hath God purposed. "All that are in their graves shall hear his voice." All the righteous, all the wicked, all that were engulfed in the sea, all that slumber on the lap of earth; all the great ones, all the multitudes of the sons of toil; all the wise and all the foolish, all the beloved and all the despised: there shall not be one single individual omitted.

My dear friend, it may be best for you to look at the question in a more personal light, *you* will not be forgotten; your separated spirit shall have its appointed place, and that body which once contained it shall have its watcher to guard it, till by the power of God it shall be restored to your spirit again, at the sounding of the last trump. You, my hearer, shall rise again. As surely as you sit here this morning, you shall stand before the once crucified Son of Man. It is not possible that you should be forgotten; you shall not be permitted to rot away into annihilation, to be left in the darkness of obscurity; you must, you shall rise, each and every one without a solitary exception. It is a wondrous truth, and yet we may not marvel at it so as to doubt it, though we may marvel at it and admire the Lord who shall bring it to pass.

Pass on. "All that are in the grave *shall hear his voice*." Hear! Why, the ear has gone! A thousand years ago a man was buried, and his ear—there is not the slightest relic of it left—all has vanished; shall that ear ever hear? Yes, for he that made it hear at the first, wrought as great a wonder then as when he shall make it hear a second time. It needed a God to make the hearing ear of the newborn babe; it shall need no more to renew the hearing ear the second time. Yes, the ear so long lost in silence shall hear! And what shall be the sound that shall startle that newly awakened and fresh fashioned ear? It shall be the voice of the Son of God; the voice of Jesus Christ Himself.

Ah, my brethren, while this teaches us the stolidity of human nature and how depraved the heart is, it also reminds you who are careless that there is no escape for you; if you will not hear the voice of Jesus now, you *must* hear it then. You may thrust those fingers into your ears to-day, but there will be no doing that in the day of the last trump, you must hear then; O that you would hear now! You must hear the summons to judgment; God grant that you may hear the summons to mercy, and become obedient to it and live. "All that are in their graves *shall* hear his voice"; whoever they may have been, they shall become subject to the power of His omnipotent command, and appear before His sovereign judgment seat.

Note the next words, "*and shall come forth*." That is to say, of course, that their bodies shall come out of the grave, out of the earth, or the water, or the air, or wherever else those bodies may be. But I think there is more than that intended by the words, "shall come forth." It seems to imply manifestation, as though all the while men were here, and when in their graves they were hidden and concealed, but as the voice of God in the thunder discovereth the forests and maketh the hinds to calve, so the voice of God in resurrection shall discover the secrets of men, and make them to bring forth their truest self into the light, to be revealed to all. The hypocrite, masked villain as he is, is not discovered now, but when the voice of Christ soundeth he shall come forth in a sense that will be horrible to him, deprived of all the ornaments of his masquerade, the vizard of his profession torn away, he shall stand before men and angels with the leprosy upon his brow, an object of universal derision, abhorred of God and despised of men.

Ah! dear hearers, are you ready to come forth even now? Would you be willing to have your hearts read out? Would you wear them on your sleeve for all to see? Is not there much about you that would not bear the light of the sun? How much more will it not bear the light of Him whose eyes are as a flame of fire, seeing all and testing all by trial which cannot err! Your coming forth on that day will be not only a reappearance from amidst the shadows of the sepulchre, but a coming forth into the light of heaven's truth which shall reveal you in meridian clearness.

And then the text goes on to say that they shall come forth as *those who have done good* and those who have done evil. From which we must gather the next truth, that death makes no change in man's character, and that after death we must not expect improvements to occur. He that is holy is holy still, and he that is filthy is filthy still. They were, when they were put into the grave, men who had done good, they rise as men who have done good; or they were, when they were interred, men who had done evil, they rise as those that have done evil. Expect, therefore, no place for repentance after this life, no opportunities for reformation, no further proclamations of mercy, or doors of hope. It is now or never with you, remember that.

Note, again, that *only two characters rise*, for indeed there are only two characters who ever lived, and, therefore, two to bury and two to rise again—those who had done good and those who had done evil. Where were those of mingled character, whose conduct was neither good nor evil, or both? There were none such. You say, do not the good do evil? May not some who are evil still do good? I answer, he that doeth good is a man who, having believed in Jesus Christ, and received the new life, doeth good in his new nature, and with his newborn spirit, with all the intensity of his heart. As for his sins and infirmities, into which by reason of his old nature he falleth, these being washed away by the precious blood of Jesus, are not mentioned in the day of account, and he rises up as a man who hath done good, his good remembered, but the evil washed away.

As for the evil, of whom it is asserted that they may do good, we answer, so they may do good in the judgment of their fellow men, and as towards their fellow mortals, but good towards God from an evil heart cannot proceed. If the fountain be defiled, every stream must be polluted also. Good is a word that may be measured according to those who use it. The evil man's good is good to you, his child, his wife, his friend, but he hath no care for God, no reverence, no esteem for the great Lawgiver. Therefore, that which may be good to you may be ill to God, because done for no right motive, even perhaps done with a wrong motive; so that the man is dishonouring God while he was helping his friend. God shall judge men by their works, but there shall be but two characters, the good and the evil; and this makes it solemn work for each man to know where he will be, and what has been the general tenor of his life, and what is a true verdict upon the whole of it.

O sirs, there are some of you, who with all your excellences and moralities, have never done good as God measures good, for you have never thought of God to honour Him, you have never even confessed that you had dishonoured Him, in fact, you have remained proudly indifferent to God's judgment of you as a sinner, and you have set yourself up as being all you should be. How shall it be possible, while you disbelieve your God, that you could do anything that can please Him? Your whole life is evil in God's sight—only evil. And as for you who fear His name, or trust you do, take heed unto your actions, I pray you, seeing that there are only those that have done good, and those that have done evil. Make it clear to your conscience, make it clear to the judgment of those who watch you (though this is of less importance), and make it clear before God, that your works are good, that your heart is right, because your outward conduct is conformed unto the law of God.

I shall not keep you much longer in the exposition, except to notice that the mode of judging is remarkable. Those who search the Scriptures know that the mode of judging at the last day will be entirely according to works. Will men be saved then for their works? no, by no means. Salvation is in every case the work and gift of grace. But the judgment will be guided by our works. It is due to those to be judged, that they should all be tried by the same rule. Now, no rule can be common to saints and sinners, except the rule of their moral conduct, and by this rule shall all men be judged. If God finds not in thee, my friend, any holiness of life whatever, neither will He accept thee. "What," saith one, "of the dying thief then?" There was the righteousness of faith in him, and it produced all the holy acts which circumstances allowed; the very moment he believed in Christ, he avowed Christ, and spoke for Christ, and that one act stood as evidence of his being a friend of God, while all his sins were washed away. May God grant you grace so to confess your sins, and believe in Jesus, that all your transgression may be forgiven you.

There must be some evidence of your faith. Before the assembled host of men there shall be no evidence given of your faith fetched from your inward feelings, but the evidence shall be found in your outward actions. It will still be, "I was an hungered, and ye gave me meat: I was thirsty, and ye gave me drink: I was a stranger, and ye took me in: naked, and ye clothed me: I was sick, and ye visited me: I was in prison, and ye came unto me." Take heed, then, as to practical godliness, and abhor all preaching which would make sanctity of life to be a secondary thing. We are justified by faith, but not by a dead faith; the faith which justifies is that which produces holiness, and "without holiness no man shall see the Lord." See ye then the two classes into which men are divided, and the stern rule by which God shall judge them, and judge yourselves that ye be not condemned with the wicked.

The different dooms of the two classes are mentioned in the text. One shall rise to *the resurrection of life*. This does not mean mere existence; they shall both exist, both exist for ever, but "life" means, when properly understood, happiness, power, activity, privilege, capacity, in fact, it is a term so comprehensive that I should need no small time to expound all it means. There is a death in life which the ungodly shall have, but ours shall be a life in life—a true life; not existence merely, but existence in energy, existence in honour, existence in peace, existence in blessedness, existence in perfection. This is the resurrection unto life.

As for the ungodly, there is a resurrection to damnation, by which their bodies and souls shall come manifestly under the condemnation of God; to use our Saviour's word, shall be *damned*. Oh, what a resurrection! and yet we cannot escape from it if we neglect the great salvation. If we could lay us down and sleep, and never wake again, oh, what a blessing it were for an ungodly man! if that grave could be the last of him, and like a dog he should never start again from slumber, what a blessing! But it is a blessing that is not yours, and never can be. Your souls must live, and your body must live. "O fear Him, I pray you, who is able to destroy both soul and body in hell. Yea, I say unto you, fear him."

II. Our time is almost spent, but I must occupy the remaining minutes in DRAWING LESSONS FROM THE TEXT.

The first is the lesson of *adoring reverence*. If it be so, that all the dead shall rise at the voice of Christ, let us worship Him. What a Saviour was He who bled upon the tree! How gloriously is He who was despised and rejected, now exalted! O brethren, if we could even get but to see the skirts of this truth, that He shall raise all the dead out of their graves, if we did but begin to perceive its grandeur of meaning, methinks we should fall at the Saviour's feet as John did when he said, "I fell at his feet as dead." Oh, what amazing power is Thine, my Lord and Master! What homage must be due to Thee! All hail, Immanuel! Thou hast the keys of death and of hell. My soul loves and adores Thee, Thou ever great enthroned Prince, the Wonderful, the Counsellor, King of kings, and Lord of lords.

The next lesson is *consolation* for our wounded spirits concerning our departed friends. We never mourn with regard to the souls of the righteous, they are for ever with the Lord. The only mourning that we permit among Christians concerns the body, which is blighted like a withered flower. When we read at funerals that famous chapter in the epistle to the Corinthians, we find in it no comfort concerning the immortal spirit, for it is not required, but we find much consolation with regard to that which is "sown in dishonour," but shall be "raised in glory." Thy dead men shall live; that decaying dust shall live again. Weep not as though thou hadst cast thy treasure into the sea, where thou couldst never find it; thou hast only laid it by in a casket, whence thou shalt receive it again brighter than before. Thou shalt look again with thine own eyes into those eyes which have spoken love to thee so often, but which are now closed in sepulchral darkness. Thy child shall see thee yet again; thou shalt know thy child; the selfsame form shall rise. Thy departed friend shall come back to thee, and having loved his Lord as thou dost, thou shalt rejoice with him in the land where they die no more. It is but a short parting, it will be an eternal meeting. For ever with the Lord, we shall also be for ever with each other. Let us comfort one another, then, with these words.

The last lesson is that of *self-examination*. If we are to rise, some to rewards and some to punishments, what shall be my position? "What shall be my position?" let each conscience ask. How do you feel, my hearers, in the prospect of rising again? Does the thought give you any gleam of joy? Does it not create a measure of alarm? If your heart trembles at the tidings, how will you bear it when the real fact is before you, and not the thought merely? What has your life been? If by that life you shall be judged, what has it been? What has been its prevailing principle up till now? Have you believed God? Do you live by faith upon the Son of God? I know you are imperfect, but are you struggling after holiness? Do you desire to honour God? This shall rule the judgment of your life; what was its end, and aim, and bent, and object? Imperfection there has been, but has there been sincerity? Has grace, divine grace, that washes sinners in the blood of Christ, proved itself to be in you by alienating you from the sins you loved, and leading you to the duties that you once neglected?

I will ask you another question: if you do not feel happy at the thought of yourself, are you quite peaceful concerning the raising of all others? Are you prepared to meet before God those whom you have sinned with among men? It is a question worthy of the sinner's thought, of what must be the terrors of men and women who will have to meet the companions of their sins! Was not this at the bottom of Dives wishing Lazarus to be sent back to the world to warn his five brethren lest they should come into the place of torment? Was not he afraid to see them there, because their recriminations would increase his misery? It will be a horrible thing for a man who has been a debauched villain to rise again and confront his victims whom his lusts dragged down to hell! How will he quail as he hears them lay their damnation at his door, and curse him for his lasciviousness! O man, your sin is not dead and buried, and the sinner whom you joined hands with in iniquity shall rise to witness against you. The crime, the guilt, the punishment, and the guilty one, shall alike live again, and you shall live for ever in remorse to rue the day in which you thus transgressed.

Another question, if it will be terrible to many to see the dead rise again, how will they endure to see Him, the Judge Himself, the Saviour? Of all men that ever lived, He is the one that you have need to be the most afraid of, because it is He whom this day you ought most to love, but whom you forget. How many times from this pulpit have I pleaded with you to yield yourselves to Jesus Christ, and how frequently have you given Him a flat denial! It may be, some of you have not quite done that, but you have postponed your decision, and said, "When I have a more convenient season I will send for thee." When He cometh, how will you answer Him? Man, how will you answer Him? How will you excuse yourselves? You would not have Him as a Saviour, but you must have Him as your Judge, to pronounce your sentence. You despised His grace, but you cannot escape His wrath. If you will but look to Jesus now, you shall find salvation in that glance, but in refusing so to do you heap up for yourself wrath when that terrible but inevitable glance shall be yours, of which the prophet says, "All the kindreds of the earth shall wail because of him." O spurn Him not, then! Despise not the Crucified! I pray you trample not upon His blood, but come to Him, that so, when you see Him on His throne you may not be afraid.

Beloved, I might have continued to ask more questions, but I shall close with these two. One of the best ways by which to learn what will be our portion in the future, is to enquire what is our portion in the present. Have you life now, I mean spiritual life—the life that grieves for sin, the life that trusts a Saviour? If so, you shall certainly have the resurrection to life. On the other hand, have you condemnation now? for he that believeth not is condemned already. Are you an unbeliever? Then you are condemned now, you shall suffer the resurrection to damnation. How can it be otherwise? Seek, then, that you may possess the life of God now by faith, and you shall have it for ever in fruition. Escape from condemnation now, and you shall escape from damnation hereafter.

God bless you all with the abundance of His salvation, for Christ's sake. Amen.

THE POWER OF CHRIST ILLUSTRATED BY THE RESURRECTION

A Sermon

Text.—"For our conversation is in heaven; from whence also we look for the Saviour, the Lord Jesus Christ: who shall change our vile body, that it may be fashioned like unto his glorious body, according to the working whereby he is able even to subdue all things unto himself."—Philippians iii. 20, 21.

I should mislead you if I called these verses my text, for I intend only to lay stress upon the closing expression, and I read the two verses because they are needful for its explanation. It would require several discourses to expound the whole of so rich a passage as this.

Beloved, how intimately is the whole of our life interwoven with the life of Christ! His first coming has been to us salvation, and we are delivered from the wrath of God through Him. We live still because He lives, and never is our life more joyous than when we look most steadily to Him. The completion of our salvation in the deliverance of our body from the bondage of corruption, in the raising of our dust to a glorious immortality, that also is wrapped up with the personal resurrection and quickening power of the Lord Jesus Christ. As His first advent has been our salvation from sin, so His second advent shall be our salvation from the grave. He is in heaven, but, as the apostle saith, "We look for the Saviour, the Lord Jesus Christ: who shall change our vile body, that it may be fashioned like unto his glorious body."

We have nothing, we are nothing, apart from Him. The past, the present, and the future are only bright as He shines upon them. Every consolation, every hope, every enjoyment we possess, we have received, and still retain because of our connection with Jesus Christ our Lord. Apart from Him we are naked, and poor, and miserable. I desire to impress upon your minds, and especially upon my own, the need of our abiding in Him. As zealous labourers for the glory of God I am peculiarly anxious that you may maintain daily communion with Jesus, for as it is with our covenant blessings, so is it with our work of faith and labour of love, everything depends upon Him. All our fruit is found in Jesus. Remember His own words, "Without me ye can do nothing." *Our* power to work comes wholly from *His* power. If we work effectually it must always be according to the effectual working of His power in us and through us.

In the text notice, first of all, *the marvel to be wrought by our Lord at His coming ;* and then gather from it, in the second place, helps to the consideration of *the power which is now at this time proceeding from Him and treasured in Him ;* and then, thirdly, *contemplate the work which we desire to see accomplished,* and which we believe will be accomplished on the ground of the power resident in our Lord.

I. First, we have to ask you to CONSIDER BELIEVINGLY THE MARVEL WHICH IS TO BE WROUGHT BY OUR LORD AT HIS COMING.

When He shall come a second time He will change our vile body and fashion it like unto His glorious body. What a marvellous change! How great the transformation! How high the ascent! Our body in its present state is called in our translation a "vile body," but if we translate the Greek more literally it is much more expressive, for there we find this corporeal frame called "the body of our humiliation." Not "this humble body," that is hardly the meaning, but the body in which our humiliation is manifested and enclosed. This body of our humiliation our Lord will transform until it is like unto His own. Here read not alone "his glorious body," for that is not the most literal translation, but "the body of his glory;" the body in which He enjoys and reveals His glory. Our Saviour had a body here in humiliation; that body was like ours in all respects except that it could see no corruption, for it was undefiled with sin; that body in which our Lord wept, and sweat great drops of blood, and yielded up His spirit, was the body of His humiliation. He rose again from the dead, and He rose in the same body which ascended up into heaven, but He concealed its glory to a very great extent, else had He been too bright to be seen of mortal eyes. Only when He passed the cloud, and was received out of sight, did the full glory of His body shine forth to ravish the eyes of angels and of glorified spirits. Then was it that His countenance became as the sun shining in its strength.

Now, beloved, whatever the body of Jesus may be in His glory, our present body which is now in its humiliation is to be conformed unto it; Jesus is the standard of man in glory. "We shall be like him, for we shall see him as he is." Here we dwell in this body of our humiliation, but it shall undergo a change, "in a moment, in the twinkling of an eye, at the last trump: for the trumpet shall sound, and the dead shall be raised incorruptible, and we shall be changed." Then shall we come into our glory, and our body being made suitable to the glory state, shall be fitly called the body of glory. We need not curiously pry into the details of the change, nor attempt to define all the differences between the two estates of our body; for "it doth not yet appear what we shall be," and we may be content to leave much to be made known to us hereafter. Yet though we see through a glass darkly, we nevertheless do see something, and would not shut our eyes to that little. We know not yet as we are known, but we do know in part, and that part knowledge is precious.

The gates have been ajar at times, and men have looked awhile, and beheld and wondered. Three times, at least, human eyes have seen something of the body of glory. The face of Moses, when he came down from the mount, shone so that those who gathered around him could not look thereon, and he had to cover it with a veil. In that lustrous face of the man who had been forty days in high communion with God, you behold some gleams of the brightness of glorified manhood. Our Lord made a yet clearer manifestation of the glorious body when He was transfigured in the presence of the three disciples. When His garments became bright and glistering, whiter than any fuller could make them, and He Himself was all aglow with glory, His disciples saw and marvelled. The face of Stephen is a third window as it were through which we may look at the glory to be revealed, for even His enemies as they gazed upon the martyr in his confession of Christ, saw his face as it had been the face of an angel. Those three transient gleams of the morning light may serve as tokens to us to help us to form some faint idea of what the body of the glory of Christ and the body of our own glory will be.

Turning to that marvellous passage in the Corinthians, wherein the veil seems to be more uplifted than it ever had been before or since, we learn a few particulars worthy to be rehearsed. The body while here below, is corruptible, subject to decay; it gradually becomes weak through old age, at last it yields to the blows of death, falls into the ground, and becomes the food of worms. But the new body shall be incorruptible, it shall not be subject to any process of disease, decay, or decline, and it shall never, through the lapse of ages, yield to the force of death. For the immortal spirit it shall be the immortal companion. There are no graves in heaven, no knell ever saddened the New Jerusalem. The body here is weak, the apostle says "it is sown in weakness;" it is subject to all sorts of infirmities in life, and in death loses all strength. It is weak to perform our own will, weaker still to perform the heavenly will; it is weak to do and weak to suffer: but it is to be "raised in power, all infirmity being completely removed." How far this power will be physical and how far spiritual we need not speculate; where the material ends and the spiritual begins we need not define; we shall be as the angels, and we have found no difficulty in believing that these pure spirits "excel in strength," nor in understanding Peter when he says that angels are "greater in power and might." Our body shall be "raised in power."

Here, too, the body is a natural or soulish body—a body fit for the soul, for the lowest faculties of our mental nature; but according to the apostle in the Corinthians, it is to be raised a spiritual body, adapted to the noblest portion of our nature, suitable to be the dwelling-place and the instrument of our new-born grace-given life. This body at present is no assistance to the spirit of prayer or praise; it rather hinders than helps us in spiritual exercises. Often the spirit truly is willing, but the flesh is weak. We sleep when we ought to watch, and faint when we should pursue. Even its joys as well as its sorrows tend to distract devotion: but when this body shall be transformed, it shall be a body suitable for the highest aspirations of our perfected and glorified humanity—a spiritual body like unto the body of the glory of Christ.

Being sinless, the body when it shall be raised again shall be painless. Who shall count the number of our pains while in this present house of clay? Truly we that are in this tabernacle do groan. Does it not sometimes appear to the children of sickness as if this body were fashioned with a view to suffering; as if all its nerves, sinews, veins, pulses, vessels, and valves, were parts of a curious instrument upon which every note of the entire gamut of pain might be produced? Patience, ye who linger in this shattered tenement, a house not made with hands awaits you. Up yonder no sorrow and sighing are met with; the chastising rod shall fall no longer when the faultiness is altogether removed. As the new body will be without pain, so will it be superior to weariness. The glory-body will not yield to faintness, nor fail through languor. Is it not implied that the spiritual body does not need to sleep, when we read that they serve God day and night in His temple?

In a word, the bodies of the saints, like the body of Christ, will be perfect; there shall be nothing lacking and nothing faulty. If saints die in the feebleness of age they shall not rise thus; or if they have lost a sense or a limb or are halt or maimed, they shall not be so in heaven, for as to body and soul "they are without fault before the throne of God." "We shall be like him," is true of all the saints, and hence none will be otherwise than fair, and beautiful, and perfect. The righteous shall be like Christ. My imagination is not able to give you a picture of the transformation; but those who will be alive and remain at the coming of the Son of God will undergo it, and so enter glory without death. "For this corruptible must put on incorruption, and this mortal must put on immortality," and therefore the bodies of living believers shall in the twinkling of an eye pass from the one state into the other; they shall be transformed from the vile to the glorious, from the state of humiliation into the state of glory, by the power of the coming Saviour.

The miracle is amazing, if you view it as occurring to those who shall be alive when Christ comes. Reflect, however, that a very large number of the saints when the Lord shall appear a second time will already be in their graves. Some of these will have been buried long enough to have become corrupt. If you could remove the mould and break open the coffin-lid, what would you find but foulness and putrefaction? But those mouldering relics are the body of the saint's humiliation, and that very body is to be transformed into the likeness of Christ's glorious body. Admire the miracle as you survey the mighty change! Look down into the loathsome tomb, and, if you can endure it, gaze upon the putrid mass; this, even this, is to be transformed into Christ's likeness. What a work is this! And what a Saviour is He who shall achieve it!

Go a little further. Many of those whom Christ will thus raise will have been buried so long that all trace of them will have disappeared; they will have melted back into the common dust of earth, so that if their bones were searched for not a vestige of them could be found, nor could the keenest searcher after human remains detect a single particle. They have slept in quiet through long ages in their lonely graves, till they have become absorbed into the soil as part and parcel of mother earth. No, there is not a bone, nor a piece of a bone left; their bodies are as much one with earth as the drop of rain which fell upon the wave is one with the sea: yet shall they be raised. The trumpet call shall fetch them back from the dust with which they have mingled, and dust to dust, bone to bone, the anatomy shall be rebuilded and then refashioned. Does your wonder grow? does not your faith accept with joy the marvel, and yet feel it to be a marvel none the less?

Son of man, I will lead thee into an inner chamber more full of wonder yet. There are many thousands of God's people to whom a quiet slumber in the grave was denied; they were cut off by martyrdom, were sawn asunder, or cast to the dogs.

Tens of thousands of the precious bodies of the saints have perished by fire, their limbs have been blown in clouds of smoke to the four winds of heaven, and even the handful of ashes which remained at the foot of the stake their relentless persecutors have thrown into rivers to be carried to the ocean, and divided to every shore. Some of the children of the resurrection were devoured by wild beasts in the Roman amphitheatres, or left a prey to kites and ravens on the gibbet. In all sorts of ways have the saints' bodies been hacked and hewn, and, as a consequence, the particles of those bodies have no doubt been absorbed into various vegetable growths, and having been eaten by animals have mingled with the flesh of beasts; but what of that?

"What of that?" say you, how can these bodies be refashioned? By what possibility can the selfsame bodies be raised again? I answer it needs a miracle to make any of these dry bones live, and a miracle being granted, impossibility vanishes. He who formed each atom from nothing can gather each particle again from confusion. The omniscient Lord of providence tracks each molecule of matter, and knows its position and history as a shepherd knows his sheep; and if it be needful to constitute the identity of the body, to regather every atom, he can do it. It may not, however, be needful at all, and I do not assert that it will be, for there may be a true identity without sameness of material; even as this my body is the same as that in which I lived twenty years ago, and yet in all probability there is not a grain of the same matter in it. God is able then to cause that the same body which on earth we wear in our humiliation, which we call a vile body, shall be fashioned like unto Christ's body. No difficulties, however stern, that can be suggested from science or physical law, shall for a single instant stand in the way of the accomplishment of this transformation by Christ the King.

What marvels rise before me! indeed, it needs faith, and we thank God we have it. The resurrection of Christ has for ever settled in our minds, beyond all controversy, the resurrection of all who are in Him; "For if we believe that Jesus died and rose again, even so them also which sleep in Jesus will God bring with him." Still it is a marvel of marvels, a miracle which needs the fulness of the deity. Of whom but God, very God of very God, could it be said that He shall change our bodies, and make them like unto His glorious body?

II. We will now pass on. Here is the point we aim at. Consider, in the second place, that THIS POWER WHICH IS TO RAISE THE DEAD IS RESIDENT IN CHRIST AT THIS MOMENT.

So saith the text, "according to the working whereby *he is able* to subdue all things unto himself." It is not some new power which Christ will take to Himself in the latter days and then for the first time display, but the power which will arouse the dead is the same power which is in Him at this moment, which is going forth from Him at this instant in the midst of His church and among the sons of men. I call your attention to this, and invite you to follow the track of the text.

First notice that all the power by which the last transformation will be wrought is ascribed to our Lord Jesus Christ now *as the Saviour.* "We look for the Saviour, the Lord Jesus." When Christ raises the dead it will be as a Saviour, and it is precisely in that capacity that we need the exercise of His power at this moment. Fix this, my brethren, in your hearts; we are seeking the salvation of men, and we are not seeking a hopeless thing, for Jesus Christ is able as a Saviour, to subdue all things, to Himself; so the text expressly tells us. It doth not merely say that as a raiser of the dead He is able to subdue all things, but as the Saviour, the Lord Jesus Christ. His titles are expressly given, He is set forth to us as the Lord, the Saviour, the Anointed, and in that capacity is said to be able to subdue all things to Himself. Happy tidings for us! My brethren, how large may our prayers be for the conversion of the sons of men, how great our expectations, how confident our efforts! Nothing is too hard for our Lord Jesus Christ: nothing in the way of saving work is beyond His power. If as a Saviour He wakes the dead in the years to come, He can quicken the spiritually dead even now.

The power of the resurrection is being put forth to-day, it is pulsing through the quickened portion of this audience, it is heaving with life each bosom that beats with love to God, it is preserving the life-courses in the souls of all the spiritual, so that they go not back to their former death in sin. The power which will work the resurrection will be wonderful, but it will be no new thing. It is everywhere to be beheld in operation in the church of God at this very moment by those who have eyes to see it; and herein I join with the apostle in his prayer "that the God of our Lord Jesus Christ, the Father of glory may give unto you the spirit of wisdom and revelation in the knowledge of him: the eyes of your understanding being enlightened; that ye may know what is the hope of his calling, and what the riches of the glory of his inheritance in the saints, and what is the exceeding greatness of his power to us-ward who believe, according to the working of his mighty power, which he wrought in Christ, when he raised him from the dead, and set him at his own right hand in the heavenly places, far above all principality, and power, and might, and dominion, and every name that is named, not only in this world, but also

E

in that which is to come: and hath put all things under his feet, and gave him to be the head over all things to the church, which is his body, the fulness of him that filleth all in all."

Note next that the terms of our text imply *that opposition may be expected to this power*, but that all resistance will be overcome. That word "subdue" supposes a force to be conquered and brought into subjection. "He is able even to subdue all things unto himself." Herein is a great wonder! There will be no opposition to the resurrection. The trumpet sound shall bring the dead from their graves, and no particle shall disobey the summons; but to spiritual resurrection there is resistance— resistance which only omnipotence can vanquish. In the conversion of sinners natural depravity is an opposing force; for men are set upon their sins, and love not the things of God, neither will they hearken to the voice of mercy.

My brethren, to remove all our fears concerning our Lord's ability to save, the word is here used, "He is able," not only to raise all things from the dead, but "*to subdue* all things to himself." Here again I would bid you take the encouragement the text presents you. If there be opposition to the gospel, He is able to subdue it. If in one man there is a prejudice, if in another man the heart is darkened with error, if one man hates the very name of Jesus, if another is so wedded to his sins that he cannot part from them, if opposition has assumed in some a very determined character, does not the text meet every case? "He is able to subdue all things," to conquer them, to break down the barriers that interpose to prevent the display of His power, and to make those very barriers the means of setting forth that power the more gloriously. "He is able even to subdue all things."

Note next, that the language of our text *includes all supposable cases*. He is able to "subdue *all* things unto himself," not here and there one, but "*all* things." Brethren, there is no man in this world so fallen, debased, depraved, and wilfully wicked, that Jesus cannot save him—not even among those who live beyond the reach of ordinary ministry. He can bring the heathen to the gospel, or the gospel to them. The wheels of providence can be so arranged that salvation shall be brought to the outcasts; even war, famine, and plague, may become messengers for Christ, for He, too, rides upon the wings of the wind.

There lived some few years ago in Perugia, in Italy, a man of the loosest morals and the worst conceivable disposition. He had given up all religion, he loathed God, and had arrived at such a desperate state of mind that he had conceived an affection for the devil, and endeavoured to worship the evil one. Imagining Satan to be the image and embodiment of all rebellion, free-thinking, and lawlessness, he deified him in his own mind, and desired nothing better than to be a devil himself. On one occasion, when a Protestant missionary had been in Perugia preaching, a priest happened to say in this man's hearing, that there were Protestants in Perugia, the city was being defiled by heretics. "And who do you think Protestants are?" said he. "They are men who have renounced Christ and worship the devil." A gross and outrageous lie was this, but it answered far other ends than its author meant. The man hearing this, thought, "Oh, then, I will go and meet with them, for I am much of their mind;" and away he went to the Protestant meeting, in the hope of finding an assembly who propagated lawlessness and worshipped the devil. He there heard the gospel, and was saved.

Behold in this and in ten thousand cases equally remarkable, the ability of our King to subdue all things unto Himself. How can any man whom God ordains to save escape from that eternal love which is as omnipresent as the deity itself? "He is able to subdue all things to himself." If His sword cannot reach the far off ones His arrows can, and even at this hour they are sharp in His enemy's hearts. No boastful Goliath can stand before our David; though the weapon which He uses to-day be but a stone from the brook, yet shall the Philistine be subdued. If there should be in this place a Deist, an Atheist, a Romanist, or even a lover of the devil, if he be but a man, mercy yet can come to him. Jesus Christ is able to subdue him unto Himself. None have gone too far, and none are too hardened. While the Christ lives in heaven we need never despair of any that are still in this mortal life—"He is able to subdue all things unto himself."

You will observe, in the text that *nothing is said concerning the unfitness of the means*. My fears often are lest souls should not be saved by our instrumentality because of faultiness in us; we fear lest we should not be prayerful enough or energetic or earnest enough; or that it should be said, "He could not do many mighty works there because of their unbelief." But the text seems to obliterate man altogether—"*He* is able to subdue all things unto himself"—that is to say, *Jesus* does it, *Jesus* can do it, will do it all. By the feeblest means He can work mightily, can take hold of us, unfit as we are for service, and make us fit, can grasp us in our folly and teach us wisdom, take us in our weakness and make us strong. My brethren, if we had to find resources for ourselves, and to rely upon ourselves, our enterprise might well be renounced, but since He is able, we will cast the burden of this work on Him, and go to Him in believing prayer, asking Him to work mightily through us to the praise of His glory, for "He is able even to subdue all things unto himself."

Note that *the ability is* said in the text to be *present with the Saviour now.* I have already pointed that out to you, but I refer to it again. The resurrection is a matter of the future, but the working which shall accomplish the resurrection is a matter of the present. "According to the working whereby he is able even to subdue all things unto himself," Jesus is as strong now as He ever will be, for He changes not. At this moment He is as able to convert souls as at the period of the brightest revival, or at Pentecost itself. There are no ebbs and flows with Christ's power. Omnipotence is in the hand that once was pierced, permanently abiding there. Oh, if we could but rouse it; if we could but bring the Captain of the host to the field again, to fight for His church, to work by His servants! What marvels should we see, for He is able. We are not straitened in Him, we are straitened in ourselves if straitened at all.

Let us cry unto our Lord, for He has but to will it and thousands of sinners will be saved; let us lift up our hearts to Him who has but to speak the word and whole nations shall be born unto Him. The resurrection will not be a work occupying centuries, it will be accomplished at once; and so it may be in this house of prayer, and throughout London, and throughout the world, Christ will do a great and speedy work to the amazement of all beholders. He will send forth the rod of His strength out of Zion, and rule in the midst of His enemies. He will unmask His batteries, He will spring His mines, He will advance His outworks, He will subdue the city of His adversaries, and ride victoriously through the Bozrah of His foes. Who shall stay His hand? Who shall say unto Him, "What doest thou?"

I wish we had time to work out the parallel which our text suggests, between the resurrection and the subduing of all things. The resurrection will be worked by the divine power, and the subduing of sinners is a precisely similar instance of salvation. All men are dead in sin, but He can raise them. Many of them are corrupt with vice, but He can transform them. Some of them are, as it were, lost to all hope, like the dead body scattered to the winds, desperate cases for whom even pity seems to waste her sighs; but He who raises the dead of all sorts, with a word can raise sinners of all sorts by the selfsame power. And as the dead when raised are made like to Christ, so the wicked when converted are made like to Jesus too. Brilliant examples of virtue shall be found in those who were terrible instances of vice; the most depraved and dissolute shall become the most devout and earnest. From the vile body to the glory-body what a leap, and from the sinner damnable in lust to the saint bright with the radiance of sanctity, what a space! The leap seems very far, but omnipotence can bridge the chasm. The Saviour, the

Lord Jesus Christ is able to do it; He is able to do it in ten thousand thousand cases, able to do it at this very moment.

III. I said I would ask you to consider, in the third place, THE WORK WHICH WE DESIRE TO SEE ACCOMPLISHED. I will not detain you however, with that consideration further than this.

Brethren, we long to see the Saviour subduing souls *unto Himself*. Not to our way of thinking, not to our church, not to the honour of our powers of persuasion, but "*unto himself*." "He is able even to subdue all things unto himself." O sinner, how I wish thou wert subdued to Jesus, to kiss those dear feet that were nailed for thee, to love in life Him Who loved thee to the death. Ah! soul, it were a blessed subjection for thee. Never subject of earthly monarch so happy in his king as thou wouldst be. God is our witness, we who preach the gospel, we do not want to subdue you to ourselves, as though we would rule you and be lords over your spirits. It is to Jesus, to Jesus only that we would have you subdued. O that you desired this subjection, it would be liberty, and peace, and joy to you!

Notice that this subjection is eminently to be desired, since it consists in transformation. Catch the thought of the text. He transforms the vile body into His glorious body, and this is a part of the subjection of all things unto Himself. But do you call that subjection? Is it not a subjection to be longed after with an insatiable desire, to be so subdued to Christ that I, a poor, vile sinner, may become like Him, holy, harmless, undefiled? This is the subjection that we wish for you, O unconverted ones. We trust we have felt it ourselves, we pray you may feel it too. He is able to give it to you. Ask it of Him at once. Now breathe the prayer, now believe that the Saviour can work the transformation in you, in you at this very moment. And, O my brethren in the faith, have faith for sinners now. While they are pleading plead for them that this subjection which is an uplifting, this conquering which is a liberating, may be accomplished in them.

For, remember again, that to be subjected to Christ is, according to our text, to be fitted for heaven. He will change our vile body and make it like the body of His glory. The body of the glory is a body fitted for glory, a body which participates in glory. The Lord Jesus can make you, sinner, though now fitted for hell, fitted for heaven, fitted for glory, and breathe into you now an anticipation of that glory, in the joy and peace of mind which His pardon will bring to you. It must be a very sad thing to be a soldier under any circumstances; to have to cut and hack and kill and subdue, even in a righteous cause, is cruel work; but to be a soldier of King Jesus is an honour and a joy. The service of Jesus is a grand service.

Brethren, we have been earnestly seeking to capture some hearts that are here present, to capture them for Jesus. It has been a long and weary siege up till this hour. We have summoned them to surrender, and opened fire upon them with the gospel, but as yet in vain. I have striven to throw a few live shells into the very heart of their city, in the form of warning and threatening and exhortation. But oh! how I wish I could burst open the gates of a sinner's heart to-day, for the Prince Emmanuel to come in. He who is at your gates is not an alien monarch, He is your rightful Prince, He is your Friend and Lover. It will not be a strange face that you will see, when Jesus comes to reign in you. When the King in His beauty wins your soul, you will think yourselves a thousand fools that you did not receive Him before. Instead of fearing that He will ransack your soul, you will open all its doors and invite Him to search each room. You will cry, "Take all, Thou blessed monarch, it shall be most mine when it is Thine. Take all, and reign and rule."

I propound terms of capitulation to you, O sinner. They are but these: yield up yourself to Christ, give up your works and ways, both good and bad, and trust in Him to save you, and be His servant henceforth and for ever. While I thus invite you, I trust He will speak through me to you and win you to Himself. I shall not plead in vain, the word shall not fall to the ground. I fall back upon the delightful consolation of our text, "He is able to subdue all things unto himself." May He prove His power this morning. Amen and Amen.

THE RESURRECTION CREDIBLE

A Sermon

Text.—"Why should it be thought a thing incredible with you, that God should raise the dead?"—Acts xxvi. 8.

CONCERNING the souls of our believing friends who have departed this life we suffer no distress, we feel sure that they are where Jesus is, and behold His glory, according to our Lord's own memorable prayer. We know but very little of the disembodied state, but we know quite enough to rest certain beyond all doubt that—

> " They are supremely blest,
>   Have done with sin, and care, and woe,
>   And with their Saviour rest."

Our main trouble is about their bodies, which we have committed to the dark and lonesome grave. We cannot reconcile ourselves to the fact that their dear faces are being stripped of all their beauty by the fingers of decay, and that all the insignia of their manhood should be fading into corruption. It seems hard that the hands and feet, and all the goodly fabric of their noble forms, should be dissolved into dust, and broken into an utter ruin. We cannot stand at the grave without tears; even the perfect Man could not restrain His weeping at Lazarus' tomb. It is a sorrowful thought that our friends are dead, nor can we ever regard the grave with love. We cannot say that we take pleasure in the catacomb and the vault. We still regret, and feel it natural to do so, that so dreadful a ban has fallen upon our race as that it should be "appointed unto all men once to die." God sent it as a penalty, and we cannot rejoice in it.

The glorious doctrine of the resurrection is intended to take away this cause of sorrow. We need have no trouble about the body, any more than we have concerning the soul. Faith being exercised upon immortality relieves us of all trembling as to the spirits of the just; and the same faith, if exercised upon resurrection, will with equal certainty efface all hopeless grief with regard to the body; for, though apparently destroyed, the body will live again—it has not gone to annihilation. That very frame which we lay in the dust shall but sleep there for a while, and, at the trump of the archangel, it shall awaken in superior beauty, clothed with attributes unknown to it while here. The Lord's love to His people is a love towards their entire manhood, He chose them not as disembodied spirits, but as men and women arrayed in flesh and blood. The love of Jesus Christ towards His chosen is not an affection for their better nature merely, but towards that also which we are wont to think their inferior part; for in His book all their members were written, He keepeth all their bones, and the very hairs of their head are all numbered.

Did He not assume our perfect manhood? He took into union with His Deity a human soul, but He also assumed a human body; and in that fact He gave us evidence of His affinity to our perfect manhood, to our flesh, and to our blood, as well as to our mind and to our spirit. Moreover, our Redeemer has perfectly ransomed both soul and body. It was not partial redemption which our Kinsman effected for us. We know that our Redeemer liveth, not only with respect to our spirit, but with regard to our body; so that though the worm shall devour its skin and flesh, yet shall it rise again because He has redeemed it from the power of death, and ransomed it from the prison of the grave.

It is a joy to think that, as Christ has redeemed the entire man, and sanctified the entire man, and will be honoured in the salvation of the entire man, so our complete manhood shall have it in its power to glorify Him. The hands with which we sinned shall be lifted in eternal adoration; the eyes which have gazed on evil shall behold the King in His beauty. Not merely shall the mind which now loves the Lord be perpetually knit to Him, and the spirit which contemplates Him will delight for ever in Him, and be in communion with Him; but this very body which has been a clog and hindrance to the spirit, and been an arch rebel against the sovereignty of Christ, shall yield Him homage with voice, and hand, and brain, and ear, and eye. We look to the time of resurrection for the accomplishment of our adoption, to wit, the redemption of the body.

Now, this being our hope, though we believe and rejoice in it in a measure, we have, nevertheless, to confess that, sometimes, questions suggest themselves, and the evil heart of unbelief cries, "Can it be true? Is it possible?" At such times the question of our text is exceedingly needful, "Why should it be thought a thing incredible with you that God should raise the dead"?

This morning, I shall *first* ask you, dear brethren, to *look the difficulty in the face ;* and, then, *secondly, we will endeavour to remove the difficulty,*—there is but one way of doing so, and that a very simple one; and then, *thirdly,* we shall have a word or two say to about *our relation to this truth.*

I. First, then, LET US LOOK THIS DIFFICULTY IN THE FACE.

We shall not, for a moment, flinch from the boldest and most plain assertion of our belief in the resurrection, but will let its difficulties appear upon the surface. Attempts have been made at different times by misguided Christians, to tone down or explain away the doctrine of the resurrection and kindred truths, in order to make them more acceptable to sceptical or philosophical minds, but this has never succeeded. No man has ever been convinced of a truth by discovering that those who profess to believe it are half ashamed of it, and adopt the tone of apology. How can a man be convinced by one who does not himself believe, for that, in plain English, is what it comes to. When we modify, qualify, and attenuate our doctrinal statements, we make concessions which will never be reciprocated, and are only received as admissions that we do not believe ourselves what we assert. By this cutting and trimming policy we shear away the locks of our strength, and break our own arm. Nothing of that kind affects me, either now or any time.

We do then really in very truth believe that the very body which is put into the grave will rise again, and we mean this literally, and as we utter it. We are not using the language of metaphor, or talking of a myth; we believe that, in actual fact, the bodies of the dead will rise again from the tomb. We admit, and rejoice in the fact, that there will be a great change in the body of the righteous man; that its materialism will have lost all the grossness and tendency to corruption which now surrounds it; that it will be adapted for higher purposes; for, whereas, it is now only a tenement fit for the soul or the lower intellectual faculties, it will then be adapted for the spirit or the higher part of our nature: we rejoice that though sown in weakness it will be raised in glory; but we nevertheless know that it will be the same body. The self-same body which is put into the grave shall rise again; there shall be an absolute identity between the body in which we die and the body in which we rise again from the dust.

But, let it be remembered that identity is not the same thing as absolute sameness of substance and continuance of atoms. We do not mention this qualification at all by way of taking off the edge from our statement, but simply because it is true. We are conscious, as a matter of fact, that we are living in the same bodies which we possessed twenty years ago; yet we are told, and we have no reason to doubt it, that perhaps not one single particle of the matter which constitutes our body now was in it twenty years ago. The changes our physical forms have undergone from infancy to manhood are very great, yet have we the same bodies. Admit the like identity in the resurrection, and it is all we ask. The body in which we die will be the same body in which we were born,—everybody admits that, though it is certainly not the same as in all its particles; nay, every particle may have been exchanged, and yet it will remain the same. So the body in which we rise will be the same body in which we die; it will be greatly changed, but those changes will not be such as to affect its identity.

Now this hope is naturally surrounded with many difficulties, because, first of all, in the great mass of the dead decay has taken place. The large majority of dead bodies have rotted and been utterly dissolved, and the larger proportion of all other bodies will probably follow them. When we see bodies that have been petrified, or mummies which have been embalmed, we think that if all bodies were preserved in that way it were easier to believe in their restoration to life; but when we break open some ancient sarcophagus, and find nothing there but a little impalpable brown powder, when we open a grave in the churchyard and find only a few crumbled pieces of bone, and when we think of ancient battle-fields where thousands have fallen, where, notwithstanding, through the lapse of years there remains not a trace of man, since the bones have so completely melted back into earth, and in some cases have been sucked up by the roots and plants, and have passed into other organisations, it certainly does seem a thing incredible that the dead should be raised.

The wonder increases when we remember in what strange places many of these bodies now may be. For the bodies of some have been left in deep mines where they will never be reached again; they have been carried by the wash and swell of tides into deep caverns of the ancient main; there they lie, far away on the pathless desert where only the vulture's eye can see them, or buried beneath mountains of fallen rock. In fact, where are not man's remains? Who shall point out a spot of earth where the crumbling dust of Adam's sons is not? Blows there a single summer wind down our streets without whirling along particles of what once was man? Is there a single wave that breaks upon any shore which holds not in solution some relic of what was once human? They lie beneath each tree, they enrich the fields, they pollute the brooks, they hide beneath the meadow grass; yet surely from anywhere, from everywhere, the scattered bodies shall return, like Israel from captivity. As certainly as God is God, our dead men shall live, and stand upon their feet, an exceedingly great army.

And, moreover, to make the wonder extraordinary beyond conception, they will rise at once, or perhaps in two great divisions. There is a passage (Rev. xx. 5, 6) which apparently teaches us that between the resurrection of the righteous and the resurrection of the wicked there will be an interval of a thousand years. Many think that the passage intends a spiritual resurrection, but I am unable to think so; assuredly the words must have a literal meaning. Hear them and judge for yourself. "But the rest of the dead lived not again until the thousand years were finished. This is the first resurrection. Blessed and holy is he that hath part in the first resurrection: on such the second death hath no power, but they shall be priests of God and of Christ, and shall reign with him a thousand years." Yet, granted that there may be this great interval, yet what a mass will be seen when the righteous rise, a "multitude that no man can number"; an inconceivable company only known to God's enumeration shall suddenly start up from "beds of dust and silent clay."

The break of a thousand years shall be as nothing in the sight of God, and shall soon be over, and then shall rise the unjust also. What teeming multitudes! where shall they stand? What plains of earth shall hold them? Shall they not cover all the solid earth even to the mountain-tops? Shall they not need to use the sea itself as a level floor for God's great assize? Before God in a moment shall they stand when the trump of the arch-angel shall ring out clear and shrill the summons for the last assize!

And then, bethink you, that this resurrection will not be a mere restoration of what was there, but the resurrection in the case of the saints will involve a remarkable advance upon anything we now observe. We put into the ground a bulb, and it rises as a golden lily; we drop into the mould a seed, and it comes forth an exquisite flower, resplendent with brilliant colours; —these are the same which we put into the earth, the same identically, but oh, how different; even thus, the bodies, which are sown in burial, are so many seeds, and they shall spring up by divine power into outgrowths, surpassing all imagination in beauty. This increases the wonder, for the Lord Jesus not only snatches the prey from between the teeth of the destroyer, but that which had become worm's meat, ashes, dust, He raises in His own sacred image. It is as though a tattered and moth-eaten garment were rent to shreds, and then by a divine word restored to its perfectness, and in addition made whiter than any fuller on earth could make it, and adorned with costly fringes and embroideries unknown to it before, and all this in a moment of time. Let it stand as a world of wonders, marvellous beyond all things: we will not, for a moment, attempt to explain it away, or pare down the angles of the truth.

One of the difficulties of believing it is this, that there are positively no full analogies in nature by which to support it. There are phenomena around us somewhat like it so that we can compare, but I believe that there is no analogy in nature upon which it would be at all fair to found an argument. For instance, some have said that sleep is the analogy of death, and that our awaking is a sort of resurrection. The figure is admirable, but the analogy is very far from perfect, since in sleep there is still life. A continuance of life is manifest to the man himself in his dreams, and to all onlookers who choose to watch the sleeper, to hear him breathe, or to watch his heart beat. But in death the body has no pulses or other signs of life left in it; it does not even remain entire as the body of the sleeper does. Imagine that the slumberer should be torn limb from limb, pounded in a mortar, and reduced to powder, and that powder mixed up with clay and mould, and then see him awaken at your call, and you would have something worth calling an analogy; but a mere sleep from which a man is startled, while it is an excellent comparison, is far enough from being the counterpart or prophecy of resurrection.

More frequently we hear mentioned the development of insects as a striking analogy. The larva is man in his present condition, the chrysalis is a type of man in his death, and the imago or perfect insect is the representation of man in his resurrection. An admirable simile, certainly, but no more, for there is life in the chrysalis; there is organisation, there is, in fact, the entire fly. No observer can mistake the chrysalis for a dead thing; take it up and you shall find everything in it that will come out of it; the perfect creature is evidently dormant there. If you could crush the chrysalis, dry up all its life juices, bruise it into dust, pass it through chemical processes, utterly dissolve it, and then afterwards call it back into a butterfly, you would have seen an analogy of the resurrection; but this is unknown to nature as yet. I find no fault with the picture, it is most instructive and interesting; but to argue from it would be childish to the last degree.

Nor is the analogy of the seed much more conclusive. The seed when put into the ground dies, and yet rises again in due season, hence the apostle uses it as the apt type and emblem of death. He tells us that the seed is not quickened except it die. What is death? Death is the resolution of an organisation into its original particles, and so the seed begins to separate into its elements, to fall back from the organisation of life into the inorganic state; but still a life germ always remains, and the crumbling organisation becomes its food from which it builds itself up again.

Is it so with dead bodies, of which not even a trace remains? Who shall discover a life germ in the putrid corpse? I shall not say there may not be some essential nucleus which better instructed beings might perceive, but I would demand where in the corrupted body it can be supposed to dwell. Is it in the brain? The brain is among the first things to disappear. The skull is empty and void. Is it in the heart? That also has a very brief duration, far briefer than the bones. Nowhere could a microscope discover any vital principle in bodies disinterred from the sod. Turn up the soil wherein the seed is buried, at anytime you will, and you will find it where you placed it, if indeed it will ever rise from the ground; but such is not the case with the man who has been buried a few hundred years; of him the last relic has probably passed beyond all recognition.

The generations to come are not more undiscoverable than those which have gone. Think of those who were buried before the flood, or drowned in that general deluge, where, I ask, have we the smallest remnant of them? Grind your corn of wheat to fine flour, and throw it to the winds, and behold corn fields rising from it, and then you will have a perfect analogy; but as yet I do not think that nature contains a parallel case. The resurrection stands alone; and, concerning it the Lord might well say, "Behold, I do a new thing in the earth." With the exception of the resurrection of our Lord, and those granted to a few persons by miracle, we have nothing in history that can be brought to bear upon the point; nor need we look there for evidence, we have a far surer ground to go upon. Here, then, is the difficulty, and a notable one it is. Can these dry bones live? Is it a credible thing that the dead should be raised?

II. How are we to meet the demands of the case? We said that in the second place we would REMOVE THE DIFFICULTY. We made no empty boast, the matter is simple. Read the text again with due emphasis, and it is done. "Why should it be thought a thing incredible with you *that* GOD *should raise the dead*"? It might seem incredible that the dead should be raised, but why should it seem incredible that GOD, the Almighty, the Infinite, should raise the dead? Grant a God, and no difficulties remain. Grant that God is, and that He is omnipotent: grant that He has said the dead shall be raised, and belief is no longer hard but inevitable. Impossibility and incredulity—both vanish in the presence of God. I believe this is the only way in which the difficulties of faith should be met: it is of no use to run to reason for weapons against unbelief, the Word of God is the true defence of faith. It is foolish to build with wood and hay when solid stones may be had. Our logic is, "God has said it," and this is our rhetoric too. If God declares that the dead shall be raised, it is not a thing incredible to us. Difficulty is not in the dictionary of the Godhead. Is anything too hard for the Lord? Heap up the difficulties, if you like, make the doctrine more and more hard for reason to compass, so long as it contains no self-evident contradiction and inconsistency, we rejoice in the opportunity to believe great things concerning a Great God.

When Paul uttered our text he was speaking to a Jew, he was addressing Agrippa, one to whom he could say, "King Agrippa, believest thou the prophets? I know that thou believest!" It was, therefore, good reasoning to use with Agrippa, to say, "Why should it be thought a thing incredible with you that God should raise the dead"? For first, as a Jew, Agrippa had the testimony of Job—"For I know that my Redeemer liveth, and that he shall stand at the latter day upon the earth: And though after my skin worms destroy this body, yet in my flesh shall I see God: whom I shall see for myself, and mine eyes shall behold, and not another; though my reins be consumed within me."

He had, also, the testimony of David, who, in the sixteenth Psalm, says, "My flesh also shall rest in hope." He had the testimony of Isaiah in the twenty-sixth chapter and the nineteenth verse, "Thy dead men shall live, together with my dead body shall they arise. Awake and sing, ye that dwell in dust: for thy dew is as the dew of herbs, and the earth shall cast out the dead." He had the testimony of Daniel in his twelfth chapter, second and third verses, where the prophet says, "And many of them that sleep in the dust of the earth shall awake, some to everlasting life, and some to shame and everlasting contempt. And they that be wise shall shine as the brightness of the firmament; and they that turn many to righteousness as the stars for ever and ever." And then again, in Hosea xiii. 14, Agrippa had another testimony where the Lord declares "I will ransom them from the power of the grave; I will redeem them from death: O death, I will be thy plagues; O grave, I will be thy destruction: repentance shall be hid from mine eyes." Thus God had plainly promised resurrection in the Old Testament Scriptures, and that fact should be quite enough for Agrippa. If the Lord has said it, it is no longer doubtful.

To us as Christians there has been granted yet fuller evidence. Remember how our Lord has spoken concerning resurrection: with no bated breath has He declared His intention to raise the dead. Remarkable is that passage in John v. 28, "Marvel not at this: for the hour is coming, in the which all that are in the graves shall hear his voice, and shall come forth; they that have done good, unto the resurrection of life; and they that have done evil, unto the resurrection of damnation." And so in chapter vi. 40, "And this is the will of him that sent me, that every one which seeth the Son, and believeth on him, may have everlasting life: and I will raise him up at the last day."

The Holy Ghost has spoken the same truth by the apostles.

In that precious and most blessed eighth chapter of the Romans, we have a testimony in the eleventh verse, "But if the Spirit of him that raised up Jesus from the dead dwell in you, he that raised up Christ from the dead shall also quicken your mortal bodies by his Spirit that dwelleth in you." I read you just now the passage from the first of Thessalonians, which is very full indeed, where we are bidden not to sorrow as those that are without hope; and you have in the Phillippians the third chapter and twenty-first verse, another proof, "Who shall change our vile body, that it may be fashioned like unto his glorious body, according to the working whereby he is able even to subdue all things unto himself." I scarcely need remind you of that grand chapter of massive argument, Corinthians the fifteenth. Beyond all doubt the testimony of the Holy Ghost is that the dead shall rise; and granted that there is an Almighty God, we find no difficulty in accepting the doctrine and entertaining the blessed hope.

At the same time it may be well to look around us, and note what helps the Lord has appointed for our faith. I am quite certain, dear friends, that there are many wonders in the world which we should not have believed by mere report, if we had not come across them by experience and observation. The electric telegraph, though it be but an invention of man, would have been as hard to believe in a thousand years ago as the resurrection of the dead is now. Who in the days of packhorses would have believed in flashing a message from England to America? When our missionaries in tropical countries have told the natives of the formation of ice, and that persons could walk across frozen water, and of ships that have been surrounded by mountains of ice in the open sea, the water becoming solid and hard as a rock all around them, the natives have refused to believe such absurd reports. Everything is wonderful till we are used to it, and resurrection owes the incredible portion of its marvel to the fact of our never having come across it in our observation—that is all. After the resurrection we shall regard it as a divine display of power as familiar to us as creation and providence now are.

Will resurrection be a greater wonder than creation? You believe that God spoke the world out of nothing. He said, "Let it be," and the world was. To create out of nothing is quite as marvellous as to call together scattered particles and refashion them into what they were before. Either work requires omnipotence, but if there be any choice between them, the resurrection is the easier work of the two. If it did not happen so often, the birth of every child into the world would astound us; we should consider a birth to be, as indeed it is, a most transcendent manifestation of divine power. It is only because we know it and see it so commonly that we do not behold the wonder-working hand of God in human births and in our continued existence. The thing, I say, only staggers us because we have not become familiar with it as yet: there are other deeds of God which are quite as marvellous.

Remember, too, that there is one thing which, though you have not seen, you have received on credible evidence, which is a part of historic truth, namely, that Jesus Christ rose again from the dead. He is to you the cause of your resurrection, the type of it, the foretaste of it, the guarantee of it. As surely as He rose you shall rise. He proved the resurrection possible by rising, nay, He proved it certain because He is the representative man; and, in rising, He rose for all who are represented by Him. "As in Adam all die, even so in Christ shall all be made alive." The rising of our Lord from the tomb should for ever sweep away every doubt as to the rising of His people. "For if the dead rise not, then is Christ not raised," but because He lives, we shall live also.

Remember also, my brethren and sisters, that you who are Christians have already experienced within yourselves as great a work as the resurrection, for you have risen from the dead as to your innermost nature. You were dead in trespasses and sins, and you have been quickened into newness of life. Of course the unconverted here will see nothing in this. The unregenerate man will even ask me what this means, and to him it can be no argument, for it is a matter of experience which one man cannot explain to his fellow. To know it ye must yourselves be born again. But, believers, ye have already passed through a resurrection from the grave of sin, and from the rottenness and corruption of evil passions and impure desires, and this resurrection God has wrought in you by a power equal to that which He wrought in Christ when He raised Him from the dead, and set Him at His own right hand in the heavenly places. To you the quickening of your spiritual nature is an assured proof that the Lord will also quicken your mortal bodies.

The whole matter is this, that our persuasion of the certainty of the general resurrection rests upon faith in God and His word. It is both idle and needless to look elsewhere. If men will not believe the declaration of God, they must be left to give an account to Him of their unbelief. My hearer, if thou art one of God's elect, thou wilt believe thy God, for God gives faith to all His chosen. If thou dost reject the divine testimony, thou givest evidence that thou art in the gall of bitterness, and thou wilt perish in it unless grace prevents. The gospel and the doctrine of the resurrection were opened up to men in all their glory to put a division between the precious and the vile. "He that is of God," saith the apostle, "heareth God's words." True faith is the visible mark of secret election. He that believeth in Christ gives evidence of God's grace towards him, but he that believes not gives sure proof that he has not received the grace of God. "But ye believe not," said Christ, "because ye are not of my sheep, as I said unto you. My sheep hear my voice, and I know them, and they follow me." Therefore this truth and other Christian truths are to be held up, maintained, and delivered fully to the whole of mankind to put a division between them, to separate the Israelites from the Egyptians, the seed of the woman from the seed of the serpent. Those whom God has chosen are known by their believing in what God has said; while those who remain unbelieving perish in their sin, condemned by the truth which they wilfully reject.

III. Thus much upon these points. Now let us consider, lastly, OUR RELATION TO THIS TRUTH.

Our first relation to this truth is this: Children of God, comfort one another with these words. You have lost those dear to you;—amend the statement—they have passed into a better land, and the body which remains behind is not lost, but put out to blessed interest. Sorrow ye must, but sorrow not as those that are without hope. I do not know why we always sing dirges at the funerals of the saints, and drape ourselves in black. I would desire, if I might have my way, to be drawn to my grave by white horses, or to be carried on the shoulders of men who would express joy as well as sorrow in their habiliments, for why should we sorrow over those who have gone to glory, and inherited immortality?

I like the old Puritan plan of carrying the coffin on the shoulders of the saints, and singing a psalm as they walked to the grave. Why not? What is there, after all, to weep about concerning the glorified? Sound the gladsome trumpet! Let the shrill clarion peal out the joyous note of victory! The conqueror has won the battle; the king has climbed to His throne. "Rejoice," say our brethren from above, "rejoice with us, for we have entered into our rest." "Blessed are the dead which die in the Lord from henceforth: yea, saith the Spirit, that they may rest from their labours and their works do follow them." If we must keep up the signs of woe, for this is natural, yet let not your hearts be troubled, for that were unspiritual. Bless God evermore that over the pious dead we sing His living promises.

Let us, in the next place, cheer our hearts in prospect of our own departure. We shall soon pass away. My brethren, we too must die; there is no discharge in this war. There is an arrow and there is an archer; the arrow is meant for my heart, and

F

the archer will take deadly aim. There is a place where you shall sleep, perhaps in a lone grave in a foreign land; or, perhaps, in a niche where your bones shall lie side by side with those of your ancestors; but to the dust return you must. Well, let us not repine, it is but for a little, it is but a rest on the way to immortality. Death is a passing incident between this life and the next,—let us meet it not only with equanimity, but with expectation, since it is not death now but resurrection to which we aspire.

Then again: are we expecting a blessed resurrection, let us respect our bodies. Let not our members become instruments of evil, let them not be defiled with sin. The Christian man must neither by gluttony nor drunkenness, nor by acts of uncleanness, in any way whatever defile his body, for our bodies are the temples of the Holy Ghost. "If any man defile that temple of God, him will God destroy." Be ye pure. In your baptism, your bodies were washed with pure water to teach you that henceforth ye must be clean from all defilement. Put away from you every evil thing. Bodies that are to dwell for ever in heaven, should not be subjected to pollution here below.

Lastly, and this is a very solemn thought, the ungodly are to rise again, but it will be to a resurrection of woe. Their bodies sinned and their bodies will be punished. "Fear him," says Christ, "who is able to destroy both soul and body in hell." He will cast both of them into a suffering which shall cause perpetually enduring destruction to them; this is terrible indeed. To slumber in the grave would be infinitely preferable to such a resurrection—"the resurrection of damnation," so the Scripture calls it; a rising "to shame and everlasting contempt," so Daniel styles it. That is a dreadful resurrection, indeed; you might be glad to escape from it. Surely it were dreadful enough for your soul to suffer the wrath of God eternally without the body having to be its companion, but so it must be; if body and soul sin, body and soul must suffer, and that for ever.

Jeremy Taylor tells us of a certain Acilius Aviola who was seized with an apoplexy, and his friends conceiving him to be dead carried him to his funeral pile, but, when the heat had warmed his body, he awoke to find himself hopelessly encircled with funeral flames. In vain he called for deliverance, he could not be rescued, but passed from torpor into intolerable torment. Such will be the dreadful awakening of every sinful body when it shall be aroused from its slumber in the grave. The body will start up to be judged, condemned, and driven from God's presence into everlasting punishment. May God grant that it may never be your case or mine, but may we believe in Christ Jesus now, and so obtain a resurrection to life eternal. Amen.

A VISIT TO THE TOMB

A SERMON

Text.—"He is not here: for he is risen, as he said. Come, see the place where the Lord lay."—Matthew xxviii. 6.

THE holy women, Mary Magdalene and the other Mary, came to the sepulchre, hoping to find there the body of their Lord, which they intended to embalm. Their intention was good; their will was accepted before God; but, for all that, their desire was not gratified, for the simple reason that it was contrary to God's design: it was at variance with even what Christ had foretold and plainly declared to them. "He is not here; for he is risen, *as he said.*" I gather from this, that there may be good desires in our hearts as believers, and we may earnestly try to carry them out, and yet we may never succeed in them, because through our ignorance we have not understood, or through our obliviousness we have happened to forget, some word of Christ that stands in our way.

I have known this to be the case in prayer. We have prayed, and we have not received, because we had no warrant in the word of God to ask the thing we did. Peradventure there was some prohibition in the Scriptures, which ought to have restrained us from offering the prayer. We have thought in our daily life, amidst the pursuits of business, that if we could gain such and such a position, then we should honour God; yet though we have sought it vigorously, and prayed about it earnestly, we have never gained it. God had never intended that we should; and, had we succeeded in compassing our own project, it might have been evil rather than advantageous, an entail of trouble instead of a heritage of joy. We were seeking great things for ourselves, we forgot that expostulation of the Lord, "Seekest thou great things for thyself? Seek them not." Do not, therefore, expect to realise all those desires which seem to you to be pure and proper. They may not happen to run in the right channel. It may be that there is a word from the Lord that forbids your ever seeing them brought to pass.

These good women found that they had lost the presence of Him Who had been their greatest delight. "He is not here,"

must have sounded like a funeral kneel to them. They expected
to find Him: He was gone. But then the grief must have been
taken out of their hearts when it was added, "He is risen." I
gather from this, that if God takes away from me any one good
thing, He will be sure to justify Himself in having so done, and
that very frequently He will magnify His grace by giving me
something infinitely better. Did Mary think it would be a good
thing to find the dead body of her Lord? Perhaps it would
have given her a kind of melancholy satisfaction. So she thought,
according to her poor judgment. The Lord took that good
thing away. But then Christ was risen, and now to hear of Him,
then presently to see Him, was not that an infinitely better thing?

Hast thou lost anything of late around which thy heart had
intertwisted all its tendrils? Thou shalt find that there is good
cause for the privation. The Lord never takes away a silver
blessing without intending to confer on us a golden gain. Depend
upon it, for wood He will give iron, and for iron He will give
brass, and for brass He will give silver, and for silver He will
give gold. All His takings are but preliminaries to larger giving.
Hast thou lost thy child? What if thou find thy Lord more
dear than ever? One smile of thy Lord will be better to thee
than all the cheerful frolics of thy child. Is He not better to
thee than ten sons? Hast thou lost the familiar companion who
once cheered thee along the vale of life? Thou shalt now by that
loss be driven closer to thy Saviour; His promises shall be more
sweet to thee, and the Blessed Spirit shall reveal His truth more
clearly to thee. Thou shalt be a gainer by thy loss.

"He is not here,"—that is sorrowful. But, "He is risen,"—
this is gladsome. Christ, the dead one, thou canst not see. Thou
canst not tenderly embalm that blessed body. But Christ, the
living one, thou shalt see; and at His feet thou shalt be able to
prostrate thyself; and from His lips thou shalt hear the gladsome
words, "Go, tell my brethren that I am risen from the dead."
That lesson may be worth your remembering. If God apply it
to your soul it may yield you rich comfort. Should the Lord
take away one joy from you, He will give you another and a
better one. "He doth not afflict willingly, nor grieve the children
of men." You never deny your children any pure gratification,
I am sure, without intending their real good. How many of
you have a way, when you put your child to a little self-denial,
of making it up to him again so that he is no loser by it. And
your heavenly Father will deal quite as gently and tenderly
with you his children.

The text contains, first, *an assurance* ; and secondly, *an invitation*.
First, an assurance: "He is not here, for he is risen;" secondly,
an invitation: "Come, see the place where the Lord lay."

I. The assurance: "He is not here, for he is risen."

Jesus Christ has really RISEN FROM THE DEAD. There is, probably, no fact in history which is so fully proven and corroborated as the fact that Jesus of Nazareth, who was nailed to the cross, and died, and was buried, did rise again. As we believe the histories of Julius Cæsar—as we accept the statements of Tacitus —we are bound on the same grounds, even as historical documents, to accept the testimony of Matthew, and Mark, and Luke, and John, and of those persons who were eye-witnesses of His death, and who saw Him after He had risen from the dead.

That Jesus Christ rose from the dead is not an allegory and a symbol, but it is a reality. There He lay dead, friend or foe to witness,—a corpse fit to be committed to the grave. Handle Him, and see. It is the very Christ you knew in life. It is the very same. Look into those eyes. Were there ever such eyes in any other human form? Behold Him! You can see the impress of sorrow on His face. Was there ever any visage so marred as His, any sorrow so real in its effects? That is the Emperor of Misery, the Prince of all Mourners, the King of Sorrow! There He lies, unmistakably the same. Now, mark the nail-prints. There went the iron through those blessed hands; and there His feet were pierced; and there is the gash that found out the pericardium, and divided the heart, and brought forth the marvellous blood and water from His side. It is He, the selfsame Christ! And the holy women lift limb by limb, and wrap Him in linen, and put the spices about Him, such as they had brought in their haste, and they lay Him down in that place—in that new tomb.

Now, let it be known and understood that our faith is that those very limbs that lay stiff and cold in death became warm with life again—that the very body which lay there, became again instinct with life, and came forth into a glorious existence. Those hands broke the piece of honeycomb and the fish in the presence of the disciples; and those lips partook thereof; and He held out those wounds and said, "Reach hither thy finger, and put it into the print of the nails;" and He bared His side, the selfsame side, and said, "Reach hither thy hand, and thrust it into my side; and be not faithless, but believing." He was no phantom, no spectre. As He Himself said, "A spirit hath not flesh and bones as ye see me have." He was real man, as much after the resurrection as He had been before; and He is real man in glory now, even as He was when here below. He has gone up: the cloud has received Him out of our sight.

The selfsame Christ who said unto Peter, "Lovest thou me?"— the selfsame Jesus who said to His disciples, "Come and dine,"

—a real man has really risen from a real death into a real life. Now, we always want to have that doctrine stated to us plainly, for though we believe it we do not always realise it; and even if we have realised it, it is good to hear it again, so as to let our minds be confirmed about it. The resurrection is as literal a fact as any other fact stated in history, and is so to be believed among us. "He is not here: for he has risen."

Pursue the narrative, beloved, and you will see that when our Lord Jesus Christ had risen on that occasion, being quickened from the slumbers of death, it was not only true that He had really risen from the sepulchre, but He had risen in order to ascend to a higher place. He now possesses that position of glory at the right hand of the Father. When He had burst the iron bonds of the grave, the disciples had this for their consolation — that He was now beyond the reach of His enemies. They could hurt Him no more. And it is so now.

He is not here, in another sense; and He is now beyond the reach of all His malignant adversaries. Does not this cheer you? It does me. No Judas can betray the Master now to be seized by Roman guards. No Pilate can now take Him and suborn justice and give Him over to be crucified, though he knows Him to be innocent. No Herod can now mock Him with his men of war: no soldiery can now spit in His dear face. Now none can buffet Him, or blindfold Him, and say unto Him, "Prophesy who it is that smote thee." The head, the dear majestic head, of Jesus can never now be crowned with thorns again, and the busy feet that ran on errands of mercy can never be pierced by the nails any more. Men shall no longer strip Him naked, and stand and exult over His agonies. He is gone beyond their reach.

Now they may rail and seek to spite Him through His people, who are the members of His body. Now they may rage; but God has set Him at His own right hand, and He is inaccessible to their malice. Oh, blessed are those words, and blessed was the pen that wrote them, and blessed was the Spirit who dictated them,—"Wherefore God also hath highly exalted him, and given him a name which is above every name; that at the name of Jesus every knee should bow, of things in heaven, and things in earth, and things under the earth; and that every tongue should confess that Jesus is Lord to the glory of God the Father."

With regard to our Lord's not being here, but having risen, it should console us to think that He is now beyond all pain, as well as beyond all personal attack. Oh, can you bear to think of Him, that He had not where to lay His head? Who among us would not have left his couch to give Him a night's rest?—ay, and have forsworn the bed for ever if we might have given Him soft repose. Would we not ourselves have taken to the hillside, and been there all night, till our head was wet with dew, if we might have gained rest for Him? He is worth ten thousand of us; and did it not seem as if it were too much for Him to have to suffer—to be homeless and houseless? He hungered, brethren; He was athirst; He was weary; he was faint. He suffered our sicknesses: we are told that He took them upon Himself. Often had He the heartache. He knew what "cold mountains and the midnight air" were to chill the body; and He knew what the bleak atmosphere and bitter privation were to freeze the soul. He passed through innumerable griefs and woes.

From the first blood-shedding at His birth, down to the last blood-shedding at His death, it seemed as if sorrow had marked Him as her peculiar child. Always was He troubled, tempted, vexed, assailed, assaulted, molested, by Satan, by wicked men, and by the evils that are without! Now there is no more of that for Him; and we are glad that He is not here for that reason. He is no child of poverty now; no carpenter's shop for Him now; no smockfrock of the peasant, woven from the top throughout, now; no mountain-side and heather for His resting place now; no jeering crowds around Him now; no stones taken up to stone Him now; no sitting on the well, weary, and saying, "Give me to drink;" no needing that He should be supplied with food when He is hungry. Now no more can there be any scourgings and flagellations. No more will He give "his back to the smiters, and his cheeks to them that plucked off the hair." No piercing His hands and His feet now; no burning thirst upon the bloody tree; no cry of "Eloi, Eloi, lama sabacthani."

God's waves and billows went over Him once, but no more can they assail Him. He was brought into the dust of death, and His soul was exceeding sorrowful once. He is beyond all that. The sea is passed, and He has come to the Fair Havens, where no storms can beat upon Him. He has reached His joy; He has entered into His rest; and He has received His reward. Brethren and sisters, let us be glad about this. Let us enter into the joy of our Lord. Let us be glad, because He is glad;—happy, because He is happy. Oh, that we might feel our hearts leaping within us, though we for a little while longer are on the field of battle, because He is clean gone from it, and now is acknowledged and adored King of kings and Lord of lords.

The fact that our Lord has risen has not only these consoling elements about it, with reference to Him, but we must remember that it is the guarantee, to every one of us who believe in Him, of our own resurrection. The apostle, in the first epistle to the Corinthians, makes the whole argument for the resurrection of

the body hinge upon this one question—did Christ rise from
the dead? If He did, then all His people must rise with Him.
He was a representative man, and as the Lord the Saviour rose,
so all His followers must. Settle the question that Christ rose,
and you have settled the question that all who are in Him,
and conformed to His image, must rise too.

That body of the dear child of God to which you bade farewell
some years ago, shall rise again. Those eyes that you closed—
those very eyes—shall see the King in His beauty in the land
that is very far off. Those ears that could not hear you when
you spoke the last tender word—those ears shall hear the eternal
melodies. That heart that grew stone cold and still, when death
laid his cold hand upon the bosom, shall beat again with newness
of life, and leap with joy amidst the festivities of the home-
bringing, when Christ the Bridegroom shall be married to His
church, the bride.

That self-same body!—Was it not the temple of the Holy
Ghost? Was it not redeemed with blood? Surely it shall rise
at the trump of the arch-angel and at the voice of God! Be
thou sure of this: be thou sure of it,—sure for thy friend and
sure for thyself. And fear not death. What is it? The grave is
but a bath wherein our body, like Esther, buries itself in spices
to make it sweet and fresh for the embrace of the glorious King
in immortality. It is but the wardrobe where we lay aside the
garment for a while. It shall come forth cleansed and purified,
with many a golden spangle on it which was not there before.
It was a work-day dress when we put it off; it will be a Sabbath
robe when we put it on, and it will be fit for Sabbath wear.
We may even long for evening to undress, if there is to be such
a waking and such a putting on of garments in the presence
of the King.

Further—not to linger too long on any one thought—let us
remember that our Lord's not being here, but having risen, has
in it this consolatory thought, that He has gone where He can
best protect our interests. He is an advocate for us. Where
should the advocate be but in the King's court? He is preparing
a place for us. Where should He be who is preparing a place,
but there—making it ready? We have a very active adversary,
who is busy accusing us. Is it not well that we have one who
can meet him face to face, and put the accuser of the brethren
to silence? He would be precious here, but He is more precious
there. He is doing more for us in heaven, than it could have
been possible for Him to do for us here below, as far as our finite
intelligence can judge, and as truly as His infinite wisdom can
pronounce. Meanwhile His absence is well compensated by the
presence of His own Spirit; and His presence there is well

consecrated by His personal administration of sacred service for our sake. All is well in heaven, for Jesus is there. The crown is safe, and the harp is secure, and the blessed heritage of each tribe of Israel all secure, for Christ is keeping it. He is, to the glory of God, the representative and preserver of His saints.

And does not this truth, that Christ is not here, but is gone, fall upon our ears with a sweet force as it constrains us to feel that this is the reason why our heart should not be here? "He is not here:" then our heart should not be here. When this text, "He is not here," was first spoken, it meant that He was not in the grave. He was somewhere on earth then. But now He is not here at all. Suppose you are very rich, and Satan whispers to you, "These are delightful gardens; this is a noble mansion; take thine ease:"—reply to him, "But *he* is not here; he is not here, he is risen; therefore I dare not put my heart where my Lord is not." Or, suppose thy family make thee very happy, and, as the little ones cluster around thee and sit around the fireside, thy heart is very glad; and though thou hast not much of this world's goods, yet thou hast enough, and thou hast a contented mind. Well, if Satan should say to thee, "Be well content, and make thy rest here," say to him, "No, *he* is not here; and I cannot feel that this is to be my abiding place. Only where Jesus is can my spirit rest." And have you lately started in life? Has the marriage day scarcely passed over? Are you just now beginning the merry days of youth, the sweet enchantment of this life's purest joy? Well, delight thyself therein, but still remember that *He* is not here, and therefore thou hast no right to say, "Soul, take thine ease!" Nowhere on earth is Christ, and therefore nowhere on earth may our heart build her nest. Oh, get thee up, my soul; get thee up, and let all thy sweetest incense go towards him who "is not here, for he is risen."

II. I must leave that point, and come with a few words to speak upon the second point, which is AN INVITATION. "Come, see the place where the Lord lay."

Not, beloved, that I am going to take you to Joseph of Arimathea's tomb. About that I shall not speak much. But I think any tomb might suffice to point the same sacred moral. In the little town of Campodolcini I once realised the tomb of Christ very vividly, in an affair which had been built for Catholic pilgrims. I was up on the hillside, and I saw written upon a wall these words, "And there was a garden." It was written in Latin. I pushed open the door of this garden. It was like any other garden; but the moment I entered there was a hand, with the words, "And in the garden there was a new tomb." Then I saw a tomb which had been newly painted, and when I came up to it I read thereon, "A new tomb wherein never man lay." I then stooped down to look inside the tomb, and I read in Latin the inscription, "Stooping down, he looked, yet went he not in." But there were the words written, "Come, see the place where the Lord lay." I went in, and I saw there, graven in stone, the napkin and the linen clothes laid by themselves. I was all alone, and I read the words, "He is not here, for he is risen," graven on the floor of the tomb. Though I dread anything scenic and histrionic and popish, yet certainly I realised very much the reality of the scene. I felt that Jesus Christ was really buried, really laid in the earth, and has really gone out of it, and it is good for us to come and see the place where Jesus lay.

Why should we see it?

Well, first, that we may see how condescending He was that ever He should lay in the grave. He that made heaven and earth, lay in the grave. He who gave light to angels' eyes, lay in the darkness three days. He slept in the darkness there. He without whom was not anything made that was made, was given up to death, and lay a victim of death there. Oh, wonder of wonders! Marvel of marvels! He, who had immortality and life within Himself, yields Himself up to the place of death!

"Come, see the place where the Lord lay," in the next place, to see how we ought to weep over the sin that laid Him there. Did I make the Saviour lie in the grave? Was it needful that before my sin could be put away, my sweet Prince, whose beauties enchant all heaven, must be chill and cold in death, and actually be laid in the tomb? Must it be so? O ye murderous sins! Ye murderous sins! Ye cruel and cursed sins! Did ye slay my Saviour? Did ye find out that tender heart? Could ye never be content until you had led Him to His death, and laid Him there? Oh, come and weep, as you see the place where the Lord lay.

"Come, see the place where the Lord lay," that you may see where you will have to lie, unless the Lord should come on a sudden. You may take the measure of that tomb, for that is where you will have to repose. It does us good to recollect, if we have great landed estates, that six feet of earth is all that will ever be our permanent freehold. We shall have to come to it—that solitary mound, with two spears length of level ground:

> " Princes, this clay must be your bed,
>   In spite of all your towers;
>   The tall, the wise, the reverent head
>   Must lie as low as ours."

There is no discharge in this war. To the dust return we must. So "Come, see the place where the Lord lay;" to see that, thou must lie there too.

But then, "Come, see the place where the Lord lay," to see what good company thou wilt have there. That is where Jesus lay: doth not that comfort thee?

> Why should the Christian fear the day
> That lands him in the tomb;
> There the dear flesh of Jesus lay,
> And left a long perfume.

What more appropriate chamber for a prince's son to go to sleep in than the prince's own tomb? There slept Emmanuel. There, my body, thou mayest be well content to sleep too! What more royal couch canst thou desire than the bosom of that same mother earth, whereon the Saviour was laid to rest a while? Think, beloved, of the ten thousand saints that have gone that way to heaven. Who shall dread to go where all the flock have gone? Thou one poor timid sheep, if thou alone hadst to go through this dark valley, thou mightest well be afraid; but, oh, in addition to thy Shepherd, who marches at the head of all the flock, listen to the footsteps of the innumerable sheep that follow Him. And some were very dear to thee, and fed in the same pasture with thee. Dost thou dread to go where they have gone? No; see the place where Jesus lay, to see what good company is to be had, though it may seem to be in a dark chamber.

"Come, see the place where the Lord lay," to see that thou canst not lie there long. It is not the place where Jesus is. He is gone, and thou art to be with Him where He is. Come and look at this tomb. There is no door to it. There was one; it was a huge rock, a monstrous stone, and none could move it. It was sealed. Seest thou not how they have set the stamp of the Sanhedrim, the stamp of the law, upon the seal, to make it sure, that none should move it?

But now, if thou wilt go to the place where Jesus lay, the seal is broken, the guards are fled, the stone is gone. Such will thy tomb be. It is true they will cover thee up, and lay on the sods of green turf. If thou art wise thou wilt prefer these things to the heavy slabs of stone they sometimes lay upon the dead. That sweet mound, with here and there a daisy, like the eye of earth looking up to heaven asking mercy, or smiling in joy of expectation—there, there wilt thou sleep; but just as in the morning thou dost but open thine eyes and the curtains are updrawn, and thou comest forth, none standing in thy way, to do the labour of the day, so, when the trump of the resurrection sounds, thou wilt rise out of thy bed in perfect liberty, none hindering thee, to see the light of the day that shall go no more down for ever. You have nothing to confine you. Bolt and bar there are none: guard and watchman none; stone and seal none. "Come, see the place where Jesus lay." I would not care to go to bed in a prison, where there stood a turnkey with his iron key to fasten me in. But I am not afraid to go to sleep in the chamber out of which I can come at the morning's call a perfectly free man! And such art thou, beloved, if thou be a believer. Thou comest to lie in a place that is open and free—a fit slumbering-place for the Lord's free men.

"Come, see the place where the Lord lay," in order to celebrate the triumph over death. If Miriam sang at the Red Sea we also may sing at Jesus' tomb. If she said, "Sing unto the Lord, for he hath triumphed gloriously," shall not we say the same? If all the hosts of Israel went out with her, the women with dances, and the strong men with their voices, in the song, so let all Israel go forth this day, and bless and praise the Lord, saying, "O death, where is thy sting? O grave, where is thy victory?" The place where Jesus lay has told us that—

> " Vain the watch, the stone, the seal!
> Christ hath burst the gates of hell."

Now let us sing unto Him, and give Him all the praise.

I was thinking to say to you, beloved, let us come and see the place where Jesus lay, to weep there for our sins; let us come and see the place where Jesus lay, to die there to our sins; let us come and see the place where Jesus lay, to be buried there with Him; let us come and see the place where Jesus lay, to rise from that place to newness of life, and find our way through resurrection-life into the ascension-life in which we shall sit in the heavenly place, and look down upon the things of earth with joyous contempt, knowing that He hath lifted us up far above them, and made us to be partakers of brighter bliss than this earth can ever know. But I will forbear.

I have done. I would to God that all here present had some share in this. You all have a share in dying. There is a tree growing out of which your coffin will be made; or perhaps it is already cut down and seasoning against the time when it shall make you a timber-suit—the last suit that you shall ever need. There is a spot of earth that must be shovelled out for you to be laid into to fill up the vacuum. And your soul shall live: your soul shall never die. Let not those who tell you of annihilation be believed for a moment. It must exist. Put it to yourself whether it shall be with the worm that never dieth and the fire that never shall be quenched, or with Christ who liveth in His glory, and who shall come a second time to give glory to His people and raise their bodies like His own. Oh, it will all hinge on this— "Dost thou believe in Jesus?" If thou dost, thou mayest welcome life and welcome death, and welcome resurrection, and welcome immortality. But if thou believest not, then a blast has come upon thee, and to thee it is terrible to die. It is terrible even to live; more terrible to die; it will be terrible to rise again; it will be terrible to be damned, and that for ever! God save thee from it, for Christ's sake! Amen.

"THE LORD IS RISEN INDEED"

A Sermon

Text.—"Why seek ye the living among the dead? He is not here, but is risen: remember how he spake unto you when he was yet in Galilee."—Luke xxiv. 5, 6.

THE first day of the week commemorates the resurrection of Christ, and, following apostolical example, we have made the first day of the week to be our Sabbath. Does not this intimate to us that the rest of our souls is to be found in the resurrection of our Saviour? Is it not true that a clear understanding of the rising again of our Lord is, through the power of the Holy Spirit, the very surest means of bringing our minds into peace? To have a part in the resurrection of Christ is to enjoy that Sabbath which remaineth for the people of God. We who have believed in the risen Lord do enter into rest, even as He also Himself is resting at the right hand of the Father. In Him we rest because His work is finished, His resurrection being the pledge that He has perfected all that is needful for the salvation of His people, and we are complete in Him. I trust this morning that some restful thoughts may, by the power of the Holy Spirit, be sown in the minds of believers while we make a pilgrimage to the new tomb of Joseph of Arimathea, and see the place where the Lord lay.

I. And, first, this morning I will speak to you upon certain INSTRUCTIVE MEMORIES which gather around the place where Jesus slept "with the rich in his death." Though He is not there, He assuredly once was there: for "He was crucified, dead, and buried." He was as dead as the dead now are, and though He could see no corruption, nor could be holden by the bands of death beyond the predestined time, yet He was in very deed most assuredly dead. No light remained in His eye, no life in His heart; thought had fled from His thorn-crowned brow, and speech from His golden mouth; He was not in mere appearance, but in reality dead—the spear-thrust decided that question once for all; therefore in the sepulchre they laid Him, a dead man, fit occupant of the silent tomb. Yet as He is not there now, but is risen, it is for us to search for memorials of His having been there. Not for the "holy sepulchre" will we contend with superstitious sectaries, but in spirit we will gather up the precious relics of the risen Redeemer.

First, He has left in the grave *the spices*. When He rose He did not bring away the costly aromatics in which His body had been wrapped, but He left them there. Joseph brought about one hundred pounds weight of myrrh and aloes, and the odour remaineth still. In the sweetest spiritual sense, our Lord Jesus has filled the grave with fragrance. It no longer smells of corruption and foul decay, but we can sing with the poet of the sanctuary—

> " Why should we tremble to convey
> These bodies to the tomb?
> There the dear flesh of Jesus lay,
> And left a long perfume."

Yonder lowly bed in the earth is now perfumed with costly spices and decked with sweet flowers, for on its pillow the truest Friend we have once laid His holy head. We will not start back with horror from the chambers of the dead, for the Lord Himself has traversed them, and where He goes no terror abides.

The Master also left His *grave-clothes* behind Him. He did not come from the tomb wrapped about with a winding-sheet; He did not wear the cerements of the tomb as the habiliments of life, but when Peter went into the sepulchre he saw the grave-clothes lying carefully folded by themselves. What if I say He left them to be the hangings of the royal bed-chamber wherein His saints fall asleep? See how He has curtained our last bed! Our dormitory is no longer bare and drear, like a prison cell, but hung around with fair white linen and comely arras—a chamber fit for the repose of princes of the blood! We will go to our last bed-chamber in peace, because Christ has furnished it for us. Or if we change the metaphor, I may say that our Lord has left those grave-clothes for us to look upon as pledges of His fellowship with us in our low estate, and reminders that as He has cast aside the death garments, even so shall we. He has risen from His couch and left His sleeping robes behind Him, in token that at our waking there are other vestures ready for us also.

What if I again change the figure, and say that as we have seen old tattered flags hung up in cathedrals and other national buildings, as the memorials of defeated enemies and victories won, so in the crypt where Jesus vanquished death His grave clothes are hung up as the trophies of His victory over death, and as assurances to us that all His people shall be more than conquerors through Him that hath loved them. "O death, where is thy sting? O grave, where is thy victory?"

Then, carefully folded up and laid by itself, our Lord left *the napkin* that was about His head. Yonder lies that napkin now. The Lord wanted it not when He came forth to life. Ye who mourn may use it as a handkerchief with which to dry your eyes. Ye widows and ye fatherless children—ye mourning brothers and ye weeping sisters—and you, ye Rachels, who will not be comforted because your children are not; here, take you this which wrapped your Saviour's face, and wipe your tears away for ever. The Lord is risen indeed, and therefore thus saith the Lord, "Refrain thy voice from weeping, and thine eyes from tears, for they shall come again from the land of the enemy," "Thy dead men shall live," O mourner—together, with the Lord's dead body, shall they arise; wherefore, sorrow not as they that are without hope, for if ye believe that Jesus died and rose again, even so them also, which sleep in Jesus, will the Lord bring with Him.

What else has the risen Saviour left behind Him? Our faith has learned to gather up memorials sweet from the couch of our Lord's tranquil slumber. Well, beloved, He left *angels* behind Him, and thus made the grave

> " A cell where angels use
> To come and go with heavenly news."

Angels were not in the tomb before, but, at His resurrection, they descended; one rolled away the stone, and others sat where the body of Jesus had lain. They were the personal attendants and bodyguard of the Great Prince, and therefore they attended Him at His rising, keeping the doorway, and answering the enquiries of His friends. Angels are full of life and vigour, but they did not hesitate to assemble at the grave, gracing the resurrection even as flowers adorn the spring. I read not that our Master has ever recalled the angels from the sepulchre of His saints; and now, if believers die as poor as Lazarus, and as sick and as despised as he, angels shall convey their souls into the bosom of their Lord, and their bodies, too, shall be watched by guardian spirits, as surely as Michael kept the body of Moses and contended for it with the foe. Angels are both the servitors of living saints and the custodians of their dust.

What else did our Well-beloved leave behind Him? He left *an open passage* from the tomb, for the stone was rolled away; doorless is that house of death. We shall, in our turn, if the Master come not speedily, descend into the prison-house of the grave. What did I say?—I called it a "prison-house," but how a prison-house, that hath no bolts or bars?—how a prison-house, that hath not even a door to close upon its occupants? Our Samson has pulled up the posts and carried away the gates of the grave with all their bars. The key is taken from the girdle of death and is held in the hand of the Prince of Life. The broken signal and the fainting watchmen are tokens that the dungeons of death can no more confine their captives. As Peter, when he was visited by the angel, found his chains fall from off him, while iron gates opened to him of their own accord, so shall the saints find ready escape at the resurrection morning. They shall sleep awhile, each one in his resting-place, but they shall rise readily, for the stone is rolled away. A mighty angel rolled away the stone, for it was very great, and when he had done the deed he sat down upon the stone. His garment was white as snow, and his face like lightning, and as he sat on the stone he seemed to say to death and hell, "Roll it back again if you can."

> " Who shall rebuild for the tyrant his prison!
> The sceptre lies broken that fell from his hands;
> His dominion is ended, the Lord is arisen;
> The helpless shall soon be released from their bands."

One thing else I venture to mention as left by my Lord in His forsaken tomb. I visited some few months ago several of the large columbaria which are to be found outside the gates of Rome. You enter a large square building, sunk in the earth, and descend by many steps, and as you descend you observe on the four sides of the great chamber, innumerable little pigeon-holes, in which are the ashes of tens of thousands of departed persons. Usually in front of each compartment prepared for the reception of the ashes stands *a lamp.* I have seen hundreds, if not thousands, of these lamps, but they are all unlit, and indeed do not appear ever to have carried light: they shed no ray upon the darkness of death. But now our Lord has gone into the tomb and illuminated it with His presence, "the lamp of His love is our guide through the gloom." Jesus has brought life and immortality to light by the gospel; and now in the dove-cotes where Christians nestle, there is light; yea, in every cemetery there is a light which shall burn through the watches of earth's night till the day break and the shadows flee away, and the resurrection morn shall dawn.

So then the empty tomb of the Saviour leaves us many sweet reflections, which we will treasure up for our instruction.

II. Our text expressly speaks of VAIN SEARCHES: "Why seek ye the living among the dead? He is not here, but is risen."

There are places where seekers after Jesus should not expect to find Him, however diligent may be their search, however sincere their desire. You cannot find a man where he is not, and there are some spots where Christ never will be discovered.

At this present moment I see many searching for Christ among the monuments of *ceremonialism*, or what Paul called "the weak and beggarly elements," for they "observe days and months and times and years." Ever since our Lord arose, Judaism and every form of symbolic ceremony have become nothing better than sepulchres. The types were of God's own ordaining, but when the substance had come, the types became empty sepulchres and nothing more. Since that time men have invented other symbols, which have not even the sanction of Divine authority, and are only dead men's graves. He Himself declared, "Neither in this mountain nor yet at Jerusalem shall men worship the Father, but the hour cometh, and now is, when the true worshippers shall worship the Father in spirit and in truth, for the Father seeketh such to worship him." Jesus has rent the veil and abolished ceremonial worship, and yet men seek to revive it, building up the sepulchres which the Lord has broken down.

Alas! there are many others who are seeking Christ as their Saviour among the tombs of *moral reformation*. Our Lord likened the Pharisees to white-washed sepulchres; inwardly they were full of dead men's bones, but outwardly they were fairly garnished. Oh, the way in which men, when they get uneasy about their souls, try to white-wash themselves. Some one gross sin is given up, not in heart, but only in appearance, and a certain virtue is cultivated not in the soul, but only in the outward act, and thus they hope to be saved, though they still remain enemies to God, lovers of sin, and greedy seekers after the wages of unrighteousness. They hope that the clean outside of the cup and the platter will satisfy the Most High, and that He will not be so severe as to look within and try their hearts.

O, Sirs, why seek ye the living among the dead? Many have sought peace for their consciences by their moral reforms, but if the Holy Spirit has truly convinced them of sin, they have soon found that they were looking for a living Christ amidst the tombs. He is not here, for He is risen. If Christ were dead, we might well say to you, "Go and do your best to be your own saviours," but while Christ is alive, He wants no help of yours— He will save you from top to bottom, or not at all. He will be Alpha and Omega to you, and if you put your hand upon His work, and think in any way that you can help Him, you have dishonoured His holy name, and He will have nothing to do with you. Seek not a living salvation amongst the sepulchres of outward formality.

Too many also are struggling to find the living Christ amidst the tombs which cluster so thickly at the foot of Sinai; they look for life to *the law*, whose ministry is death. Men think that they are to be saved by keeping God's commandments. They are to do their best, and they conceive that their sincere endeavours will be accepted, and they will thus save themselves. This self-righteous idea is diametrically opposed to the whole spirit of the gospel. The gospel is not for you who can save yourselves, but for those who are lost. If you can save yourselves, go and do it, and do not mock the Saviour with your hypocritical prayers. Go and stumble among the tombs of ancient Israel, and perish as they did in the wilderness, for into rest Moses and the law can never lead you. The gospel is for sinners who cannot keep the law for themselves, who have broken it, and incurred its penalty, who know that they have done so, and confess it. For such, a living Saviour has come that He may blot out their transgressions. Seek not salvation by the works of the law, for by them shall no flesh living be justified. By the law is the knowledge of sin, and nothing more; but righteousness, peace, life, salvation, come by faith in the living Lord Jesus Christ, and by no other means. "Believe in the Lord Jesus Christ, and thou shalt be saved;" but if thou goest about to establish thine own righteousness, thou shalt surely perish, because thou hast rejected the righteousness of Christ.

Others there are who seek the living Jesus among the tombs, by looking for something good in *human nature*, in their own natural hearts and dispositions. I can see you now, for I have known you long, and this has always been your folly, you will go into the charnel house of your own nature, and say, "Is Jesus here?" Beloved, you are sad and depressed, and I do not wonder. Look at yonder dry bones and bleaching skeletons. See that heap of rottenness, that mass of corruption, that body of death—can you bear it? "Ah," say you, "I am a wretched man indeed, but I long to find some good thing in my flesh!" O beloved, you sigh in vain, you might as well rake hell over to find heaven in it, as look into your own carnal nature to find consolation. Behold ye this day, God has abandoned the old nature, and given it up to death.

Under the old law, circumcision was the putting away of the filth of the flesh, as though after this filth were gone the flesh might perhaps be bettered, but now, under the new covenant, we have a far deeper symbol, for "know ye not, that so many of us as were baptized into Jesus Christ were baptized into his death? Therefore we are buried with him by baptism into death: that like as Christ was raised up from the dead by the glory of the Father, even so we also should walk in new-ness of life." The old man is buried, as a dead thing out of which no good can come. "Knowing this, that our old man is crucified with him, that the body of sin might be destroyed, that hence-forth we should not serve sin." God does not attempt to renew the old carnal mind, but to make us new creatures in Christ Jesus.

Yet again, too many have tried to find Christ amidst the gloomy catacombs of the world's *philosophy*. For instance, on the Sabbath day they like to have a sermon full of thought—thought being in the modern meaning of it something beyond, if not opposite to, the simple teaching of the Bible. If a man tells his people what he finds in the Scriptures he is said to "talk platitudes;" but if a man amuses his people with his own dreams, however opposed they may be to God's thoughts, he is a "thinking man," a "highly intellectual preacher." There be some who love above all things the maunderings of day-dreamers, and the crudities of sceptics. If they can hear what an infidel Professor has said against inspiration, if they can be indulged with the last new blasphemy, some hearers feel that they are making advances in that higher culture, which is so much vaunted now-a-days. But, believe me, the bat-haunted caves of false philosophy and pretended science have been searched again and again, but salvation dwells not in them. In Paul's day there were Gnostics who tracked all the winding passages of vainglorious learning, but they only discovered "another gospel which was not another."

The world by wisdom knew not God. After roaming amid the dreary catacombs of philosophy, we come back to breathe the fresh air of the living Word, and concerning the mazes of science, we gasp out the sentence,—"He is not there." Reason has not found Him in her deepest mining, not speculation in her highest soaring, though indeed He is not far from any one of us. Athens has her unknown God, but in the simple gospel God is known in the person of Jesus. Socrates and Plato hold up their candles, but Jesus is the sun. Our moderns cavil and dispute, and yet a living Christ is among us converting sinners, cheering saints, and glorifying God.

How anxiously do I wish that you who have been searching for salvation in any of these directions would give up the hopeless task, and understand that Christ is nigh you, and if you with the heart believe on Him, and with the mouth confess Him, you shall be saved. "Look unto me and be ye saved, all the ends of the earth; for I am God, and beside me there is none else:" this is His cry to you. "Faith cometh by hearing, and hearing by the word of God." "Believe in the Lord Jesus

Christ and thou shalt be saved." Jesus is living still, and able to save to the uttermost. All you have to do is simply to turn the glance of your faith towards Him: by that faith He becomes yours, and you are saved, but oh, seek not the living among the dead, for He is risen.

III. We will again change our strain and consider, in the third place, UNSUITABLE ABODES. The angels said to the women, "He is not here, but is risen." As much as to say—since He is alive He does not abide here. The living Christ might have sat down in the tomb—He might have made the sepulchre His resting place, but it would not have been appropriate; and so He teaches us to-day that Christians should dwell in places appropriate to them. Ye are risen in Christ, ye ought not to dwell in the grave. I shall now speak to those who, to all intents and purposes, live in the sepulchre, though they are risen from the dead.

Some of these are excellent people, but their temperament, and perhaps their mistaken convictions of duty, lead them to be perpetually *gloomy and desponding*. They hope they have believed in Christ, but they are not sure; they trust that they are saved, but they would not be presumptuous enough to say so. They do not dare to be happy in the conviction that they are accepted in the Beloved. They love the mournful string of the harp, they mourn an absent God. They hope that the divine promises will be fulfilled: they trust that, perhaps, one of these days they may come forth into light, and see a little of the brightness of the Lord's love, but now they are ready to halt, they dwell in the valley of the shadow of death, and their soul is sore burdened.

Dear friend, do you think this is a proper condition for a Christian to be in? I am not going to deny your Christianity for a moment, for I have not half so much doubt about that as you have; I have a better opinion of you than you have of yourself. The most trembling believer in Jesus is saved, and your little faith will save you; but do you really think that Christ meant you to stay where you are, sitting in the cold and silent tomb, amid the dust and ashes? Why keep underground? why not come into the Master's garden where the flowers are breathing perfume? Why not enjoy the fresh light of full assurance, and the sweet breath of the Spirit's comforting influences? It was a madman who dwelt among the tombs, do not imitate him. Do not say I have been such a sinner, that this is all I deserve to enjoy; for if you talk of deserving, you have left the gospel altogether. I know you believe in Jesus, and you would not give up your hope for all the world: you feel after all that

He is a precious Christ to you; come, then, rejoice in Him, though you cannot rejoice in yourself.

Come, beloved, come out of this dreary vault, leave it at once! Though you have lien among the pots, yet now shall ye be as the wings of a dove covered with silver, and her feathers with yellow gold. Your Master comes to you now, and says, "O my dove, that art in the clefts of the rocks, in the secret places of the stairs, let me see thy countenance, let me hear thy voice; for sweet is thy voice, and thy countenance is comely." Members of the body of a risen Saviour, will ye lie in the grave still? Arise ye, and come away! Doubt no longer. O believer, what cause hast thou to doubt thy God? Has he ever lied unto thee? Question no longer the power of the precious blood. Why shouldst thou doubt it? Is it not able to cleanse thee from sin? No longer enquire as to whether thou art saved or can be—if thou believest thou art as safe as Christ is. Thou canst no more perish than Christ can if thou art resting in Him—His word has pledged it, His honour is involved in it, He will surely bring thee unto the promised rest; therefore be glad.

Another sort of people seem to dwell among the tombs: I mean Christians—and I trust real Christians—who are very, very *worldly*. It is no sin for a man to be diligent in business, but it is a grievous fault when diligence in business destroys fervency in spirit, and when there is no serving of God in daily life. A Christian man should be diligent so as to provide things honest in the sight of all men, but there be some who are not content with this. They have enough, but they covet more, and when they have more, they still stretch their arms like seas to grasp in all the shore, and their main thought is not God, but gold; not Christ, but wealth. O brethren, brethren, permit me earnestly to rebuke you, lest you receive a severe rebuke in providence in your own souls. Christ is not here! He dwells not in piles of silver. You may be very rich, and yet not find Christ in it all; and you might be poor, and yet if Christ were with you you would be happy as the angels. He is not here, He is risen! A marble tomb could not hold Him, nor could a golden tomb have contained Him. Let it not contain you. Unwrap the cerements of your heart; cast all your care on God who careth for you. Let your conversation be in heaven. Set not your affection on things on the earth, but set it upon things above, where Christ sitteth at the right hand of God.

Once more on this point, a subject more grievous still, there are some professors who live in the dead-house of *sin*. Yet they say that they are Christ's people. Nay, I will not say they live in it, but they do what, perhaps, is worse—they go to sin to find their pleasures. I suppose we may judge of a man more by that wherein he finds his pleasure than by almost anything else. A man may say, "I do not habitually frequent the gaieties of the world; I am not always found where sin is mixed with mirth, and where worldlings dance upon the verge of hell, but I go there now and then for a special treat."

I cannot help quoting the remark of Rowland Hill, who, when he met with a professor who went to the theatre, a member of his church, said to him, "I understand you attend the theatre." "No," he said, "I only go for a treat now and then." "Ah," said Mr. Hill, "that makes it all the worse. Suppose that somebody said, 'Mr. Hill is a strange being, he eats carrion.' I am asked, 'Is it true, Mr. Hill, that you live on carrion?' 'No, I do not habitually eat carrion, but I have a dish of it now and then just for a treat.' Why, you would think I was nastier than I should have been if I had eaten it ordinarily." There is much force in the remark. If anything that verges on the unclean and lascivious is a treat to you, why then your very heart is unclean, and you are seeking your pleasure and comfort among the dead.

There are some things that men take pleasure in now-a-days that are only fit to make idiots laugh, or else to cause angels to weep. Do be choice, Christian men and women, in your company. You are brothers to Christ; will you consort with the sons of Belial? You are heirs of perfection in Christ, you are even now arrayed in spotless linen, and you are fair and lovely in the sight of God; you are a royal priesthood, you are the elect of mankind; will you trail your garments in the mire and make yourselves the sport of the Philistines? Will you consort with the beggarly children of the world? No; act according to your pedigree and your newborn nature, and never seek the living among the dead. Jesus was never there—go not there yourselves. He loved not the noise and turmoil of the world's pleasures; He had meat to eat of another kind. God grant you to feel the resurrection life strong within your spirits.

IV. But I pass on from that. In the fourth place, I want to warn you against UNREASONABLE SERVICES. Those good people to whom the angels said, "He is not here, but is risen," were bearing a load, and what were they carrying? What is Joanna carrying, and her servants, and Mary, what are they carrying? Why, white linen, and what else? Pounds of spices, the most precious they could buy. What are they going to do? Ah, if an angel could laugh, I should think he must have smiled as he found they were coming to embalm Christ. "Why he is not here: and, what is more, he is not dead, he does not want any embalming, he is alive."

You might have seen all over England on Good Friday, and also on this Easter Sunday, crowds of people, I have no doubt very sincere people, coming to embalm Christ. They tolled a bell because He was dead, and they hung crape over what they call their altars because He was dead, and they fasted and sung sad hymns over their dead Saviour. I bless the Lord my Redeemer is not dead, and I have no bells to toll for Him either. He is risen, He is not here! Here they come, crowds of them with their white linen, and their precious spices to wrap a dead Christ up in. Are the men mad? But say they, we were only acting it over again. Oh, was that it? Practical charades was it? Acting the glorious atonement of Calvary as a play! Then I accuse the performers of blasphemy before the throne of the eternal God who hears my words; I charge them with profanity in daring to rehearse in mimicry that which was once done and done for ever, and is never to be repeated.

No, I cannot suppose they meant to mimic the great sacrifice, and, therefore, I conclude that they thought their Saviour to be dead, and so they said, "Toll the bell for Him! Kneel down and weep before His image on a cross." If I believed Jesus Christ died on Good Friday, I would feast all day long because His death is over; as He has ordained the high festival of the Lord's Supper to be His commemoration, I would follow His bidding, and keep no fast. Who would sit down and whine over a friend once dead if you knew Him to be restored to life and exalted in power? Why toll a bell for a living friend? However, I condemn not the good people any more than the angels condemned those holy women, only they may take their spices home and their white linen too, for Jesus is alive, and does not want them.

In other ways a great many fussy people do the same thing. See how they come forward in defence of the gospel. It has been discovered by geology and by arithmetic, that Moses was wrong. Straightway many go out to defend Jesus Christ. They argue for the gospel, and apologize for it, as if it were now a little out of date, and we must try to bring it round to suit modern discoveries and the philosophies of the present period. That seems to me exactly like coming up with your linen and precious spices to wrap Him in. Take them away. I question whether Butler and Paley have not both of them created more infidels than they ever cured, and whether most of the defences of the gospel are not sheer impertinences. The gospel does not want defending. If Jesus Christ is not alive, and cannot fight His own battles, then Christianity is in an evil case. But He is, and we have only to preach His gospel in all its naked simplicity, and the power that goes with it will be the evidence of its divinity.

No other evidence will ever convince mankind. Apologies and defences are well intended no doubt, so was the embalming well intended by these good women, but they are of small value. Give Christ room, give His preachers space and opportunities to preach the gospel, and let the truth be brought out in simple language, and you will soon hear the Master say, "Take away the spices, take away the linen! I am alive, I do not want these."

We see the same kind of thing in other good people who are sticklers for old-fashioned, stereotyped ways—they must have everything conducted exactly as it used to be conducted one hundred or two hundred years ago. Puritanic order must be maintained, and there must be no divergence, and the way of putting the gospel must be exactly the same way in which it was put by good old Dr. So-and-so, and in the pulpit there must be the most awful dreariness that can possibly be compassed, and the preacher must be devoutly dull, and all the worship must be serenely proper—lots of spices and fine linen to wrap a dead Christ up in. I delight to break down conventional proprieties. It is a grand thing to put one's foot right through merely human regulations, because life cannot be strapped down by regulations fit only for the dead. Mr. Hill went to Scotland to preach the gospel, and they said he rode on the back of all order and decorum. Then said he, "I will call my pair of horses by those names, and make it true." It was true; no doubt, he did ride on the back of order and decorum, but then he drew souls to Christ with those two strange steeds, and his breaking through rules enabled him to get at men and women who never would have been got at in any other way. Be ready to set Christ at liberty, and give His servants liberty to serve Him as the Spirit of God shall guide them.

V. I wanted to speak, last of all, upon THE AMAZING NEWS which these good women received:—"He is not here, but he is risen." This was amazing news to His enemies. They said, "We have killed Him—we have put Him in the tomb; it is all over with Him." A-ha! Scribe, Pharisee, Priest, what have you done? Your work is all undone, for He is risen! It was amazing news for Satan. He no doubt dreamed that he had destroyed the Saviour, but He is risen! What a thrill went through all the regions of hell! What news it was for the grave! Now was it utterly destroyed, and death had lost his sting! What news it was for trembling saints. "He is risen indeed." They plucked up courage, and they said, "The good cause is the right one still, and it will conquer, for our Christ is still alive at its head. It was good news for sinners. Ay, it is good news for every sinner here. Christ is alive; if you seek Him He will be found of you.

He is not a dead Christ to whom I point you to-day. He is risen; and He is able to save to the uttermost them that come unto God by Him. There is no better news for sad men, for distressed, desponding, and despairing men, than this—the Saviour lives, able still to save and willing to receive you to His tender heart. This was glad news, beloved, for all the angels and all the spirits in heaven, glad news indeed for them. And this day it shall be glad news to us, and we will live in the power of it by the help of His Spirit, and we will tell it to our brethren that they may rejoice with us, and we will not despair any longer. We will give way no more to doubts and fears, but we will say to one another, "He is risen indeed; therefore let our hearts be glad." The Lord bless you, and in coming to His table, as I trust many of His people will come, let us meet our risen Master. Amen.

THE POWER OF THE RISEN SAVIOUR

A Sermon

Text.—"And Jesus came and spake unto them, saying, All power is given unto me in heaven and in earth. Go ye therefore, and teach all nations, baptizing them in the name of the Father, and of the Son, and of the Holy Ghost: teaching them to observe all things whatsoever I have commanded you: and, lo, I am with you alway, even unto the end of the world. Amen."—Matthew xxviii. 18–20.

THE change from "the man of sorrows" before His crucifixion to the "Lord over all" after His resurrection is very striking. Before His passion He was ·well known by His disciples, and appeared only in one form, as the Son of man, clad in the common peasant's garment without seam, woven from the top throughout; but after He had risen from the dead He was on several occasions unrecognized by those who loved Him best, and is once at least described as having appeared to certain of them "under another form." He was the same person, for they saw His hands and His feet, and Thomas even handled Him, and placed his finger in the print of the nails; but yet it would seem that some gleams of His glory were at times manifested to them, a glory which had been hidden during His previous life, save only when He stood on the Mount of Transfiguration.

Before His death, His appearances were to the general public —He stood in the midst of Scribes and Pharisees and publicans and sinners, and preached the glad tidings; but now He appeared only to His disciples, sometimes to one, at another time to two, on one occasion to about five hundred brethren at once, but always to His disciples, and to them only. Before His death His preaching was full of parable, plain to those who had understanding, but often dark and mysterious even to His own followers, for it was a judgment from the Lord upon that evil generation that seeing they should not see, and hearing they should not perceive. Yet with equal truth we may say that our Lord before His death brought down His teaching to the comprehension of the uninstructed minds which listened to it, so that many of the deeper truths were slightly touched upon because they were not able to bear them as yet.

Till His crucifixion He veiled the effulgence of many truths, but after His resurrection He spake no more in parables, but introduced His disciples into the inner circle of the great doctrines of the kingdom, and as it were showed Himself face to face to them. Before His death the Lord Jesus was ever with His followers, and even the secret places of His retirement were known to them, but after He had risen He came and went among them at irregular intervals. Where He was during many of those forty days who among us can tell? He was seen in the garden upon Olivet, He walked to Emmaus, He comforted the assembly at Jerusalem, He showed Himself again to the disciples at the Sea of Tiberias, but where went He when, after the various interviews, He vanished out of their sight?

They were in the room alone, the doors were shut, and suddenly He stood in the midst of them; again He called to them from the sea-beach, and on landing they found a fire of coals kindled, and fish laid thereon, and bread; His appearings were strange, and His disappearings equally so. Everything betokened that, after He had risen from the dead, He had undergone some marvellous change, which had revealed in Him that which had been concealed before, though still His identity was indisputable.

It was no small honour to have seen our risen Lord while yet He lingered here below. What must it be to see Jesus as He is now! He is the same Jesus as when He was here; yonder memorials as of a lamb that has been slain assure us that He is the same man. Glorified in heaven His real manhood sits, and it is capable of being beheld by the eye, and heard by the ear, but yet how different. Had we seen Him in His agony, we should all the more admire His glory. Dwell with your hearts very much upon Christ crucified, but indulge yourselves full often with a sight of Christ glorified. Delight to think that He is not here, for He is risen; He is not here, for He has ascended; He is not here, for He sits at the right hand of God, and maketh intercession for us. Let your souls travel frequently the blessed highway from the sepulchre to the throne. As in Rome there was a *Via Sacra* along which returning conquerors went from the gates of the city up to the heights of the Capitol, so is there another *Via Sacra* which you ought often to survey, for along it the risen Saviour went in glorious majesty from the tomb of Joseph of Arimathea up to the eternal dignities of his Father's right hand. Your soul will do well to see her dawn of hope in His death, and her full assurance of hope in His risen life.

To-day my business is to show, as far as God the Spirit may help me, first, *Our Lord's resurrection power !* and secondly, *Our Lord's mode of exercising the spiritual part of that power so far as we are concerned.*

I. OUR LORD'S RESURRECTION POWER. "All power is given unto me in heaven and in earth." At the risk of repeating myself, I should like to begin this head by asking you to remember last Sabbath morning's sermon, when we went to Gethsemane, and bowed our spirits in the shade of those grey olives, at the sight of the bloody sweat. What a contrast between that and this! There you saw the weakness of man, the bowing, the prostrating, the crushing of the manhood of the Mediator; but here you see the strength of the God-man:—He is girt with omnipotence, though still on earth when He spoke these words He had received a privilege, honour, glory, fulness and power which lifted Him far above the sons of men. He was, as Mediator, no more a sufferer, but a sovereign; no more a victim, but a victor; no more a servant, but the monarch of earth and heaven. Yet He had never received such power if He had not endured such weakness. All power had never been given to the Mediator if all comfort had not been taken away. He stooped to conquer. The way to His throne was downward. Mounting upon steps of ivory, Solomon ascended to his throne of gold; but Our Lord and Master descended that He might ascend, and went down into the awful deeps of agony unutterable that all power in heaven and earth might belong to Him as our Redeemer and Covenant Head.

Now think a moment of these words, "*All power.*" Jesus Christ has given to Him by His Father, as a consequence of His death, "all power." It is but another way of saying that the Mediator possesses omnipotence, for omnipotence is but the Latin of "all power." What mind shall conceive, what tongue shall set in order before you, the meaning of all power? We cannot grasp it; it is high, we cannot attain unto it. Such knowledge is too wonderful for us. The power of self-existence, the power of creation, the power of sustaining that which is made, the power of fashioning and destroying, the power of opening and shutting, of overthrowing or establishing, of killing and making alive, the power to pardon and to condemn, to give and to withhold, to decree and to fulfil, to be, in a word, "head over all things to his church,"—all this is vested in Jesus Christ our Lord. We might as well attempt to describe infinity, or map the boundless as to tell what "all power" must mean; but whatever it is, it is all *given* to our Lord, all lodged in those hands which once were fastened to the wood of shame, all left with that heart which was pierced with the spear, all placed as a crown upon that head which was surrounded with a coronet of thorns.

"All power *in heaven*" is His. Observe that! Then He has the power of God, for God is in heaven, and the power of God emanates from that central throne. Jesus, then, has divine power. Whatever Jehovah can do Jesus can do. If it were His will to speak another world into existence, we should see to-night a fresh star adorning the brow of night. Were it His will at once to fold up creation like a worn out vesture, lo the elements would pass away, and yonder heavens would be shrivelled like a scroll. The power which binds the sweet influences of the Pleiades and looses the bands of Orion is with the Nazarene, the Crucified leads forth Arcturus with his sons. Angelic bands are waiting on the wing to do the bidding of Jesus of Nazareth, and cherubim and seraphim and the four living creatures before the throne unceasingly obey Him. He Who was despised and rejected of men now commands the homage of all heaven, as "God over all, blessed for ever."

"All power in heaven" relates to the providential skill and might with which God rules everything in the universe. He holds the reins of all created forces, and impels or restrains them at His will, giving force to law, and life to all existence. The old heathen dreamed of Apollo as driving the chariot of the sun and guiding its fiery steeds in their daily course, but it is not so: Jesus is Lord of all. He harnesses the winds to His chariot, and thrusts a bit into the mouth of the tempest, doing as He wills among the armies of heaven and the inhabitants of this lower world. From Him in heaven emanates the power which sustains and governs this globe, for the Father hath committed all things into His hands. "By him all things consist."

"All power" must include—and this is a practical point to us—all the power of the Holy Ghost. In the work which lies nearest our heart the Holy Spirit is the great force. It is He that convinces men of sin, and leads them to a Saviour, gives them new hearts and right spirits, and plants them in the church, and then causes them to grow and become fruitful. The power of the Holy Ghost goes forth among the sons of men according to the will of our Lord. As the anointing oil poured upon Aaron's head ran down his beard, and bedewed the skirts of his garments, so the Spirit which has been granted to him without measure flows from Him to us. He hath the residue of the Spirit, and according to His will the Holy Ghost goeth forth into the church, and from the church into the world, to the accomplishment of the purposes of saving grace. It is not possible that the church should fail for want of spiritual gifts or influence while her heavenly Bridegroom has such overflowing stores of both.

All the power of the sacred Trinity, Father, Son, and Spirit, is at the command of Jesus, who is exalted far above all principality, and power, and might, and dominion, and every name that is named, not only in this world, but in that which is to come.

Our Lord also claimed that all power had been given to him *on earth*. This is more than could be truly said by any mere man; none of mortal race may claim all power in heaven, and when they aspire to all power on earth it is but a dream. Universal monarchy has been strained after; it has seldom, if ever, been attained; and when it seemed within the clutch of ambition it has melted away like a snowflake before the sun. Indeed, if men could rule all their fellows, yet they would not have all power on earth, for there are other forces which scorn their control. Fell diseases laugh at the power of men. The King of Israel, when Naaman came to him to be recovered of his leprosy, cried, "Am I God, to kill and to make alive, that this man doth send unto me to recover a man of his leprosy?" He had not all power. Winds and waves, moreover, scorn mortal rule. It is not true that even Britannia rules the waves. The proudest princes have been made to feel by sickness, and pain, and death that after all they were but men; and oftentimes their weaknesses have been such as to make the more apparent the truth that power belongeth unto God, and unto God alone, so that when He entrusts a little of it to the sons of men, it is so little that they are fools if they boast thereof. See ye, then, before us a wonder. A man who has power over all things on earth without exception, and is obeyed by all creatures, great and small, because the Lord Jehovah has put all things under His feet.

For our purposes it will be most important for us to remember that our Lord has "all power" over the minds of men, both good and bad. He calleth whomsoever He pleaseth into His fellowship, and they obey. Having called them, He is able to sanctify them to the highest point of holiness, working in them all the good pleasure of His will with power. The saints can be so influenced by our Lord, through the Holy Ghost, that they can be impelled to the divinest ardours, and elevated to the sublimest frames of mind. Often do I pray, and I doubt not the prayer has come from you too, that God would raise up leaders in the church, men full of faith and of the Holy Ghost, standard-bearers in the day of battle. The preachers of the gospel who preach with any power are few; still might John say, "Ye have not many fathers." More precious than the gold of Ophir are men who stand out as pillars of the Lord's house, bulwarks of the truth, champions in the camp of Israel. How few are our apostolic men! We want again Luthers, Calvins, Bunyans, Whitfields, men fit to mark eras, whose names breathe terror in our foemen's ears. We have dire need of such. Where are they? Whence will they come to us? We cannot tell in what farmhouse or village smithy, or school house such men may be, but our Lord has them in store. They are the gifts of Jesus Christ to the church, and will come in due time. Let us believe in the power of Jesus to give us valiant men and men of renown, and we little know how soon He will supply them.

Since all power on earth is lodged in Christ's hands, He can also clothe any and all of His servants with a sacred might, by which their hands shall be sufficient for them in their high calling. Without bringing them forth into the front ranks He can make them occupy their appointed stations till He comes, girt with a power which shall make them useful. My brother, the Lord Jesus can make you eminently prosperous in the sphere in which He has placed you; my sister, your Lord can bless the little children who gather at your knee through your means. You are very feeble, and you know it, but there is no reason why you should not be strong in Him. If you look to the strong or strength, He can endue you with power from on high, and say to you as to Gideon, "Go in this thy might." Your slowness of speech need not disqualify you, for He will be with your mouth as with Moses. Your want of culture need not hinder you, for Shamgar with his oxgoad smote the Philistines, and Amos, the prophet, was a herdsman.

Like Paul, your personal presence may be despised as weak, and your speech as contemptible, but yet like him you may learn to glory in infirmity, because the power of God doth rest upon you. Ye are not straitened in the Lord, but in yourselves, if straitened at all. You may be as dry as Aaron's rod, but He can make you bud and blossom, and bring forth fruit. You may be as nearly empty as the widow's cruse, yet will He cause you still to overflow towards His saints. You may feel yourself to be as near sinking as Peter amid the waves, yet will He keep you from your fears. You may be as unsuccessful as the disciples who had toiled all night and taken nothing, yet He can fill your boat till it can hold no more. No man knows what the Lord can make of him, nor what He may do by him, only this we do know assuredly that "all power" is with Him by whom we were redeemed, and to whom we belong.

Oh, believers, resort ye to your Lord, to receive out of His fulness grace for grace. Because of this power we believe that if Jesus willed He could stir the whole church at once to the utmost energy. Does she sleep? His voice can awaken her. Does she restrain prayer? His grace can stimulate her to devotion. Has she grown unbelieving? He can restore her ancient faith. Does she turn her back in the day of battle, troubled with scepticisms and doubts? He can restore her unwavering confidence in the gospel, and make her valiant till all her sons shall be heroes of faith and put to flight the armies of the aliens.

Let us believe, and we shall see the glory of God. Let us believe, I say, and once again our conquering days shall come, when one shall chase a thousand, and two shall put ten thousand to flight. Never despair for the church; be anxious for her, and turn your anxiety into prayer, but be hopeful evermore, for her Redeemer is mighty and will stir up His strength. "The Lord of Hosts is with us; the God of Jacob is our refuge." Degenerate as we are, there standeth one among us whom the world seeth not, whose shoe's latchet we are not worthy to unloose: He shall again baptise us with the Holy Ghost and with fire, for "all power is given unto him."

It is equally true that all power is given unto our Lord over the whole of mankind, even over that part of the race which rejects and continues in wilful rebellion. He can use the ungodly for his purposes. We have it on inspired authority that Herod and Pilate, with the Gentiles and the people of Israel, were gathered together to do whatsoever the Lord's hand and counsel determined before to be done. Their utmost wickedness did but fulfil the determinate counsel of God. Thus doth He make wrath of man to praise Him, and the most rebellious wills to be subservient to His sacred purposes. Jesu's kingdom ruleth over all. The powers of hell and all their hosts, with the kings of the earth, and the rulers set themselves and take counsel together, and all the while their rage is working out His designs. Little do they know that they are but drudges to the King of Kings, scullions in the kitchen of His imperial palace. All things do His bidding, His will is not thwarted, His resolves are not defeated; the pleasure of the Lord prospers in His hands.

By faith I see Him ruling and overruling on land and sea, and in all deep places. Guiding the decisions of parliaments, dictating to dictators, commanding princes, and ruling emperors. Let Him but arise, and they that hate Him shall flee before Him; as smoke is driven, so will He drive them away; as wax melteth before the fire, so shall all His enemies perish at His presence.

As to *sinful men* in general, the Redeemer has power over their minds in a manner wonderful to contemplate. At the present moment we very much deplore the fact that the current of public thought runs strongly towards Popery, which is the

H

alias of idolatry. Just as, in Old Testament history, the people of Israel were always breaking away after their idols, so is it with this nation. The Israelites were cured of their sin for a little while, so long as some great teacher· or judge had power among them, but at his death they turned aside to worship the queen of heaven or the calves of Bethel, or some other visible symbols. So it is now. Men are mad after the idols of old Rome. Well, what next? Are we despairing? God forbid that we should ever despond while all power is in the hand of Jesus.

A great philosopher has told us that it is absurd to suppose that prayer can have any effect upon the events of life; but God has only to visit the nation with some judgment severely felt by all and your philosopher will become as quiet as a mouse. The current of thought can readily be turned by our Lord; He can as easily manage it as the miller controls the stream which flows over His wheel, or rushes past it. The times are safe in our Redeemer's management, He is mightier than the devil, the Pope, the infidel, and the ritualist, all put together. All glory be to Him who has all power in earth and heaven.

So too, our Lord can give, and He does give to the people an inclination to hear the gospel. Never be afraid of getting a congregation when the gospel is your theme. Jesus, who gives you a consecrated tongue, will find willing ears to listen to you. At His bidding deserted sanctuaries grow crowded, and the people throng to hear the joyful sound. Ay, and He can do more than that, for He can make the word powerful to the conversion of thousands. He can constrain the frivolous to think, the obstinately heretical to accept the truth, and those who set their faces like a flint to yield to His gracious sway. He has the key of every human heart; He openeth, and no man shutteth; He shutteth, and no man openeth. He will clothe His word with power and subdue the nations thereby. It is ours to proclaim the gospel, and to believe that no man is beyond the saving power of Jesus Christ. Doubly dyed, yea, sevenfold steeped in the scarlet dye of vice, the sinner may be cleansed, and the ringleader in vice may become a pattern of holiness. The Pharisee can be converted—was not Paul? Even priests may be saved, for did not a great multitude of the priests believe? There is no man in any conceivable position of sin, who is beyond the power of Christ. He may be gone to the uttermost in sin, so as to stand on the verge of hell, but if Jesus stretch out His pierced hand, he will be plucked like a brand out of the burning.

Brethren, we have no doubts, we entertain no fears, for every moment of time is bringing on the grand display of the power of Jesus. We preach to-day, and some of you despise the gospel;

we bring Christ before you, and you reject Him; but God will change His hand with you before long, and your despisings and your rejectings will then come to an end, for that same Jesus who went from Olivet, and ascended into heaven, will so come in like manner as He was seen to go up into heaven. He will descend with matchless pomp and power, and this astonished world which saw Him crucified shall see Him enthroned; and in the self same place where men dogged His heels and persecuted Him, they shall crowd around Him to pay Him homage, for He must reign, and put His enemies under His feet. This same earth shall be gladdened by His triumphs which once was troubled with His griefs.

And more. You may be dead before the Lord shall come, but you will know that all power is His, for at the blast of His trumpet your bodies shall rise again to stand before His terrible judgment seat. You may have resisted Him here, but you will be unable to oppose Him then; you may despise Him now, but then you must tremble before Him. "Depart ye cursed," will be to you a terrible proof that He has "all power," if you will not now accept another and a sweeter proof of it by coming unto Him who bids the labouring and heavy laden partake of His rest. "Kiss the Son, lest he be angry, and ye perish from the way, when his wrath is kindled but a little. Blessed are all they that put their trust in him."

II. I have, secondly, by your patience, to show OUR LORD'S USUAL MODE OF EXERCISING HIS GREAT SPIRITUAL POWER. Brethren, the Lord Jesus might have said, "All power is given to Me in heaven and earth; take ye then your swords and slay all these My enemies who crucified Me." But He had no thoughts of revenge. He might have said, "These Jews put Me to death, therefore go ye straightway to the Isles and to Tarshish and preach, for these men shall never taste of My grace," but no, He expressly said, "beginning at Jerusalem," and bade His disciples first preach the Gospel to His murderers. In consequence of His having "all power" His servants were bidden to disciple all nations. My brethren, the method by which Jesus proposes to subdue all things unto Himself appears to be utterly inadequate. To teach, to make disciples, to baptize these disciples, and to instruct them further in the faith! Good Master, are these the weapons of our warfare? Are these thy battleaxe and weapons of war? Not thus do the princes of this world contemplate conquest, for they rely on monster guns, ironclads, and engines of death-doing power. Yet what are these but proofs of their weakness? Had they all power in themselves they would not need such instruments. Only He who has all power can work His bidding by a word, and dispense with all force but that of love.

Mark that *teaching and preaching are the Lord's way of displaying His power*. To-day they tell us that the way to save souls is to rig out an altar with different coloured silks and satins, variable according to the almanack, and to array priests in garments of divers colours, "of divers colours of needlework, on both sides, meet for the necks of them that take the spoil," and to make men wear petticoats, dishonourable to their sex. With these ribbons and embroideries, joined with incense-burning, posturing, and incantations, souls are to be saved! "Not so," saith the Master, but "Go ye into all the world, and preach the gospel to every creature." Preaching and teaching and baptizing the disciples are Christ's way, and priestcraft is not Christ's way. If Christ had ordained sacramental efficacy it would succeed, but He has ordained nothing of the kind; His mandate is—All power is given unto Me in heaven and earth, go ye, therefore, disciple, baptize, and then still further instruct in the name of the Triune God.

My brethren, remember who the men were who were sent on this errand. The eleven who were foremost were mostly fishermen. Does the omnipotent Jesus choose fishermen to subdue the world? He does, because He needs no help from them; all power is His. We must have an educated ministry, they tell us; and by "an educated ministry" they mean, not the ministry of a man of common sense, clear head and warm heart, deep experience, and large acquaintance with human nature, but the ministry of mere classical and mathematical students, theorists, and novices, more learned in modern infidelities than in the truth of God. Our Lord, if he had wished to employ the worldly-wise, might certainly have chosen an eleven in Corinth or in Athens who would have commanded general respect for their attainments, or He could have found eleven learned rabbis near at home; but He did not want such men: their vaunted attainments were of no value in His eyes. He chose honest, hearty men who were childlike enough to learn the truth, and bold enough to speak it when they knew it.

The church must get rid of her notion that she must depend on the learning of this world. Against a sound education we cannot have a word to say, especially an education in the Scriptures, but to place learned degrees in the place of the gift of the Holy Spirit, or to value the present style of so-called culture above the spiritual edification of our manhood, is to set up an idol in the house of the living God. The Lord can as well use the most illiterate man as the most learned, if so it pleaseth Him. "Go ye," he said, "ye fishermen, go ye, and teach all nations." Carnal reason's criticism on this is,—a feeble method to be worked out by feebler instruments!

Now let it be noted here that the work of preaching the gospel, which is Christ's way of using His power among men, is based only upon His having that power. Hearken to some of my brethren; they say, "You must not preach the gospel to a dead sinner, because the sinner has no power." Just so, but our reason for preaching to him is that all power is given unto Jesus, and He bids us preach the gospel to every creature. I tell you this, if my Lord and Master should bid me go to-morrow to Norwood cemetery and bid the dead to rise I would do it with as much pleasure as I now preach the gospel to this congregation; and I would do it for the same reason which now leads me to urge the unregenerated to repent and be converted; for I regard men as being dead in sin, and yet I tell them to live, because my Master commands me do so: that I am right in thus acting is proved by the fact that while I am preaching sinners do live; blessed be His name, thousands of them have been quickened into life.

Ezekiel had to cry, "Ye dry bones, live." What a foolish thing to say! But God justified His servant in it, and an exceeding great army stood upon their feet in what was once a large charnel house. Joshua's men were bidden to blow their trumpets around Jericho—a most absurd thing to blow a trumpet to fetch city walls down—but they came down for all that. Gideon's men were bidden simply to carry lamps within their pitchers, and to break their pitchers, and stand still and cry aloud, "The sword of the Lord and of Gideon,"—a most ridiculous thing to hope by this means to smite the Midianites,—but they were smitten, for God never sends His servants on a fool's errand. It pleases God by the foolishness of preaching to accomplish His divine purpose, not because of the power of preaching, nor the power of the preacher, nor any power in those preached to, but because "all power" is given unto Christ "in heaven and in earth," and He chooses to work by the teaching of the Word.

Our business, then, is just this. We are to teach, or as the Greek word has it, to make disciples. Our business is, each one according to the grace given, to tell our fellow men the gospel, and to try and disciple them to Jesus. When they become disciples, our next duty is to give them the sign of discipleship, by "baptising them." That symbolic burial sets forth their death in Jesus to their former selves and their resurrection to newness of life through Him. Baptism enrols and seals the disciples, and we must not omit or misplace it. When the disciple is enrolled, the missionary is to become the pastor, "teaching them to observe all things whatsoever I have commanded you."

The disciple is admitted into the school by obeying the Saviour's command as to baptism, and then he goes on to learn, and as he learns he teaches others also. He is taught obedience, not to some things, but to all things which Christ has commanded. He is put into the church not to become a legislator or a deviser of new doctrines and ceremonies, but to believe what Christ tells him, and to do what Christ bids him.

I would close this sermon very practically. The greater part of my congregation at this time consists of persons who have believed in Jesus, who have been baptised, and have been further instructed. You believe that Jesus has all power, and that He works through the teaching and preaching of the gospel, and therefore I wish to press you with a home question. How much are you doing as to teaching all nations? This charge is committed to you as well as to me; for this purpose are we sent into the world; ourselves receivers that we may be afterwards distributors. How much have you distributed?

Dear brother, dear sister, to how many have you told the story of redemption by the blood of Jesus? You have been a convert now for some time: to whom have you spoken of Jesus, or to whom have you written? Are you distributing as best you can the words of others if you are not capable of putting words together yourself? Do not reply, "I belong to a church which is doing much." That is not to the point. I am speaking of that which you are personally doing. Jesus did not die for us by proxy, but He bore our sins in His own body on the tree. I ask then, what are you personally doing? Are you doing anything at all? "But I cannot go for a missionary," says one. Are you sure you cannot? I have been long looking for a time when numbers of you will feel that you must go to preach the gospel abroad, and will relinquish comforts and emoluments for the Lord's sake. There can be no greater honour to a church than to have many sons and daughters bearing the brunt of the battle for the Lord.

Lo, I set up a standard among you this day, let those whose hearts God has touched rally to it without delay. The heathen are perishing; they are dying by millions without Christ, and Christ's last command to us is "Go ye, teach all nations:" are you obeying it? "I cannot go," says one, "I have a family and many ties to bind me at home." My dear brother, then, I ask you, are you going as far as you can? Do you travel to the utmost length of the providential tether which has fastened you where you are? Can you say "Yes." Then, what are you doing to help others to go? As I was thinking over this discourse, I reflected how very little we were most of us doing towards sending the gospel abroad.

We are, as a church, doing a fair share for our heathen at home, and I rejoice at the thought of it; but how much a year do you each give to foreign missions? I wish you would put down in your pocket-book how much you give per annum for missions, and then calculate how much per cent. it is of your income. There let it stand—"Item: Gave to the collection last April . . . 1s." One shilling a year towards the salvation of the world. Perhaps it will run thus—"Item: Income £5,000, annual subscription to mission £1." How does that look? I cannot read your hearts, but I could read your pocket-books and work a sum in proportion. I suggest that you do it yourselves, while I also take a look at my own expenditure. Let us all see what more can be done for the spread of the Redeemer's kingdom, for all power is with Him; and when His people shall be stirred up to believe in that power, and to use the simple but potent machinery of the preaching of the Gospel to all nations, then God, even our own God shall bless us, and all the ends of the earth shall fear Him. Amen.

CHRIST THE DESTROYER OF DEATH

A Sermon

Text.—"The last enemy that shall be destroyed is death."—1 Cor. xv. 26.

During four previous Sabbaths we have been following our Lord and Master through His great achievements: we have seen Him as the end of the law, as the conqueror of Satan, as the overcomer of the world, as the creator of all things new, and now we behold Him as the destroyer of death. In this and in all His other glorious deeds let us worship Him with all our hearts.

May the Spirit of God lead us into the full meaning of this, which is one of the Redeemer's grandest characters.

To the text itself then: *death is an enemy: death is an enemy to be destroyed: death is an enemy to be destroyed last:*—"the last enemy that shall be destroyed is death."

I. DEATH AN ENEMY. *It was so born,* even as Haman the Agagite was the enemy of Israel by his descent. Death is the child of our direst foe, for "sin when it is finished bringeth forth death." "Sin entered into the world and death by sin." Now, that which is distinctly the fruit of transgression cannot be other than an enemy of man. Death was introduced into the world on that gloomy day which saw our fall, and he that had the power of it is our arch enemy and betrayer, the devil: from both of which facts we must regard it as the manifest enemy of man. Death is an alien in this world, it did not enter into original design of the unfallen creation, but its intrusion mars and spoils the whole. It is no part of the Great Shepherd's flock, but it is a wolf which cometh to kill and to destroy.

Geology tells us that there was death among the various forms of life from the first ages of the globe's history, even when as yet the world was not fitted up as the dwelling of man. This I can believe and still regard death as the result of sin. If it can be proved that there is such an organic unity between man and the lower animals that they would not have died if Adam had not sinned, then I see in those deaths before Adam the antecedent consequences of a sin which was then uncommitted. If by the merits of Jesus there was salvation before He had offered his atoning sacrifice I do not find it hard to conceive that the foreseen demerits of sin may have cast the shadow of death over the long ages which came before man's transgression. Of that we know little, nor is it important that we should, but certain is it that as far as this present creation is concerned death is not God's invited guest, but an intruder whose presence mars the feast. Man in his folly welcomed Satan and sin when they forced their way into the high festival of Paradise, but he never welcomed death: even his blind eyes could see in that skeleton form a cruel foe. As the lion to the herds of the plain, as the scythe to the flowers of the field, as the wind to the sere leaves of the forest, such is death to the sons of men. They fear it by an inward instinct because their conscience tells them that it is the child of their sin.

Death is well called an enemy for *it does an enemy's work* towards us. For what purpose doth an enemy come but to root up, and to pull down, and to destroy? Death tears in pieces that comely handiwork of God, the fabric of the human body, so marvellously wrought by the fingers of divine skill. Casting this rich embroidery into the grave among the armies of the worm, to its fierce soldiery death divideth "to every one a prey of divers colours, of divers colours of needlework"; and they ruthlessly rend in pieces the spoil. This building of our manhood is a house fair to look upon, but death the destroyer darkens its windows, shakes its pillars, closes its doors and causes the sound of the grinding to cease. Then the daughters of music are brought low, and the strong men bow themselves. This Vandal spares no work of life, however full of wisdom, or beauty, for it looseth the silver cord and breaketh the golden bowl. Lo, at the fountain the costly pitcher is utterly broken, and at the cistern the well-wrought wheel is dashed in pieces. Death is a fierce invader of the realms of life, and where it comes it fells every good tree, stops all wells of water, and mars every good piece of land with stones. See you a man when death has wrought his will upon him, what a ruin he is! How is his beauty turned to ashes, and his comeliness to corruption. Surely an enemy hath done this.

Look, my brethren, at the course of death throughout all ages and in all lands. What field is there without its grave? What city without its cemetery? Whither can we go to find no sepulchres? As the sandy shore is covered with the up-castings of the worm, so art thou, O earth, covered with those grass-grown hillocks beneath which sleep the departed generations of men. And thou, O sea, even thou, art not without thy dead! As if the earth were all too full of corpses and they jostled each other in their crowded sepulchres, even into thy caverns, O mighty main, the bodies of the dead are cast. Thy waves must become defiled with the carcases of men, and on thy floor must lie the bones of the slain! Our enemy, death, has marched as it were with sword and fire ravaging the human race. Neither Goth, nor Hun, nor Tartar could have slain so universally all that breathed, for death has suffered none to escape. Everywhere it has withered household joys and created sorrow and sighing; in all lands where the sun is seen it hath blinded men's eyes with weeping. The tear of the bereaved, the wail of the widow, and the moan of the orphan—these have been death's war music, and he has found therein a song of victory.

The greatest conquerors have only been death's slaughtermen, journeymen butchers working in his shambles. War is nothing better than death holding carnival, and devouring his prey a little more in haste than is his common wont.

Death has done the work of an enemy to those of us who have as yet escaped his arrows. Those who have lately stood around a new-made grave and buried half their hearts can tell you what an enemy death is. It takes the friend from our side, and the child from our bosom, neither does it care for our crying. He has fallen who was the pillar of the household; she has been snatched away who was the brightness of the hearth. The little one is torn out of its mother's bosom though its loss almost breaks her heart-strings; and the blooming youth is taken from his father's side though the parent's fondest hopes are thereby crushed. Death has no pity for the young and no mercy for the old; he pays no regard to the good or to the beautiful. His scythe cuts down sweet flowers and noxious weeds with equal readiness. He cometh into our garden, trampleth down our lilies and scattereth our roses on the ground; yea, and even the most modest flowers planted in the corner, and hiding their beauty beneath the leaves that they may blush unseen, death spieth out even these, and cares nothing for their fragrance, but withers them with his burning breath. He is thine enemy indeed, thou fatherless child, left for the pitiless storm of a cruel world to beat upon, with none to shelter thee. He is thine enemy, O widow, for the light of thy life is gone, and the desire of thine eyes has been removed with a stroke. He is thine enemy, husband, for thy house is desolate and thy little children cry for their mother of whom death has robbed thee.

Even *those who die* may well count death to be their enemy: I mean not now that they have risen to their seats, and, as disembodied spirits, behold the King in His beauty, but aforetime while death was approaching them. He seemed to their trembling

flesh to be a foe, for it is not in nature, except in moments of
extreme pain or aberration of mind, or of excessive expectation
of glory, for us to be in love with death. It was wise of our
Creator so to constitute us that the soul loves the body and the
body loves the soul, and they desire to dwell together as long
as they may, else had there been no care of self-preservation,
and suicide would have destroyed the race.

When death cometh even to the good man he cometh as an
enemy, for he is attended by such terrible heralds and grim
outriders as do greatly scare us.

> " Fever with brow of fire;
> Consumption wan; palsy, half-warmed with life,
> And half a clay-cold lump; joint-torturing gout,
> And ever-gnawing rheum; convulsion wild;
> Swoln dropsy; panting asthma; apoplex
> Full forged."

None of these add to the aspect of death a particle of beauty.
He comes with pains and griefs; he comes with sighs and tears.
Clouds and darkness are round about him, an atmosphere laden
with dust oppresses those whom he approaches, and a cold
wind chills them even to the marrow. He rides on the pale
horse, and where his steed sets its foot the land becomes a desert.
By the footfall of that terrible steed the worm is awakened to
gnaw the slain. When we forget other grand truths and only
remember these dreadful things, death is the king of terrors
to us. Hearts are sickened and reins are loosened, because of
him.

If you think for a few moments of this enemy, you will observe
some of his points of character. He is the *common* foe of all God's
people, and the enemy of all men: for however some have been
persuaded that they should not die, yet is there no discharge
in this war; and if in this conscription a man escapes the ballot
many and many a year till his grey beard seems to defy the
winter's hardest frost, yet must the man of iron yield at last.
It is appointed unto all men once to die. The strongest man
has no elixir of eternal life wherewith to renew his youth amid
the decays of age: nor has the wealthiest prince a price wherewith to bribe destruction. To the grave must thou descend, O
crowned monarch, for sceptres and shovels are akin. To the
sepulchre must thou go down, O mighty man of valour, for
sword and spade are of like metal. The prince is brother to the
worm, and must dwell in the same house. Of our whole race
it is true, "Dust thou art, and unto dust shalt thou return."

Death is also a *subtle* foe, lurking everywhere, even in the

most harmless things. Who can tell where death has not prepared his ambuscades? He meets us both at home and abroad;
at the table he assails men in their food, and at the fountain he
poisons their drink. He waylayeth us in the streets, and he seizeth
us in our beds; he rideth on the storm at sea, and he walks with
us when we are on our way upon the solid land. Whither can
we fly to escape from thee, O death, for from the summit of the
Alps men have fallen to their graves, and in the deep places
of the earth where the miner goeth down to find the precious
ore, there hast thou sacrificed many a hecatomb of precious
lives. Death is a subtle foe, and with noiseless footfalls follows
close at our heels when least we think of him.

He is an enemy *none of us will be able to avoid*, take what by-
paths we may, nor can we escape from him when our hour is
come. Into this fowler's nets, like the birds, we shall all fly;
in his great *seine* must all the fishes of the great sea of life be
taken when their day is come. As surely as sets the sun, or as
the midnight stars at length descend beneath the horizon, or
as the waves sink back into the sea, or as the bubble bursts,
so must we all early or late come to our end, and disappear
from earth to be known no more among the living.

Sudden too, full often, are the assaults of this enemy.

> " Leaves have their time to fall,
>   And flowers to wither at the north wind's breath,
>   And stars to set—but all,
>   Thou hast all seasons for thine own, O Death!"

Such things have happened as for men to die without an instant's
notice; with a psalm upon their lips they have passed away;
or engaged in the daily business they have been summoned
to give in their account. We have heard of one who, when the
morning paper brought him news that a friend in business
had died, was drawing on his boots to go to his counting-house,
and observed with a laugh that as far as he was concerned,
he was so busy he had no time to die. Yet, ere the words were
finished, he fell forward and was a corpse. Sudden deaths are
not so uncommon as to be marvels if we dwell in the centre
of a large circle of mankind. Thus is death a foe not to be
despised or trifled with. Let us remember all his characteristics,
and we shall not be inclined to think lightly of the grim enemy
whom our glorious Redeemer has destroyed.

II. Secondly, let us remember that death is AN ENEMY TO
BE DESTROYED. Remember that our Lord Jesus Christ has
already wrought a great victory upon death so that He has
delivered us from life long bondage through its fear. He has not

yet *destroyed death*, but He has gone very near to it, for we are told that He has "abolished death and hath brought life and immortality to light through the gospel." This surely must come very near to having destroyed death altogether.

In the first place, our Lord has subdued death in the very worst sense by having delivered His people from spiritual death. "And you hath he quickened who were dead in trespasses and sins." Once you had no divine life whatever, but the death of original depravity remained upon you, and so you were dead to all divine and spiritual things; but now, beloved, the Spirit of God, even He that raised up Jesus Christ from the dead, has raised you up into newness of life, and you have become new creatures in Christ Jesus. In this sense death has been subdued.

Our Lord in His life-time also conquered death by restoring certain individuals to life. There were three memorable cases in which at His bidding the last enemy resigned his prey. Our Lord went into the ruler's house, and saw the little girl. who had lately fallen asleep in death, around whom they wept and lamented: He heard their scornful laughter, when He said, "She is not dead but sleepeth," and He put them all out and said to her, "Maid, arise!" Then was the spoiler spoiled, and the dungeon door set open. He stopped the funeral procession at the gates of Nain, whence they were carrying forth a young man, "the only son of his mother, and she was a widow," and he said, "Young man, I say unto thee arise." When that young man sat up and our Lord delivered him to his mother, then again was the prey taken from the mighty. Chief of all when Lazarus had laid in the grave so long that his sister said, "Lord, by this time he stinketh," when, in obedience to the words, "Lazarus come forth!" forth came the raised one with his grave-clothes still about him, but yet really quickened, then was death seen to be subservient to the Son of man. "Loose him and let him go," said the conquering Christ, and death's bonds were removed, for the lawful captive was delivered. When at the Redeemer's resurrection many of the saints arose and came out of their graves into the holy city then was the crucified Lord proclaimed to be victorious over death and the grave.

Still, brethren, these were but preliminary skirmishes and mere foreshadowings of the grand victory by which death was overthrown. The real triumph was achieved upon the cross—

> " He hell in hell laid low;
> Made sin, He sin o'erthrew:
> Bow'd to the grave, destroy'd it so,
> And death, by dying, slew."

When Christ died He suffered the penalty of death on the behalf of all His people, and therefore no believer now dies by way of punishment for sin, since we cannot dream that a righteous God would twice exact the penalty for one offence. Death since Jesus died is not a penal infliction upon the children of God: as such He has abolished it, and it can never be enforced. Why die the saints then? Why, because their bodies must be changed ere they can enter heaven. "Flesh and blood" as they are "cannot inherit the kingdom of God." A divine change must take place upon the body before it will be fit for incorruption and glory; and death and the grave are, as it were, the refining pot and the furnace by means of which the body is made ready for its future bliss. Death, it is true thou art not yet destroyed, but our living Redeemer has so changed thee that thou art no longer death, but something other than thy name! Saints die not now, but they are dissolved and depart. Death is the loosing of the cable that the bark may freely sail to the fair havens. Death is the fiery chariot in which we ascend to God: it is the gentle voice of the Great King, who cometh into his banqueting hall, and saith, "Friend, come up higher." Behold, on eagle's wings we mount, we fly, far from this land of mist and cloud, into the eternal serenity and brilliance of God's own house above. Yes, our Lord has abolished death. The sting of death is sin, and our great Substitute has taken that sting away by His great sacrifice. Stingless, death abides among the people of God, but it so little harms them that to them "it is not death to die."

Further, Christ vanquished death and thoroughly overcame him when He rose. What a temptation one has to paint a picture of the resurrection, but I will not be led aside to attempt more than a few touches. When our great Champion awoke from His brief sleep of death and found Himself in the withdrawing-room of the grave, He quietly proceeded to put off the garments of the tomb. How leisurely He proceeded! He folded up the napkin and placed it by itself, that those who lose their friends might wipe their eyes therewith; and then He took off the winding sheet and laid the graveclothes by themselves that they might be there when His saints come thither, so that the chamber might be well furnished, and the bed ready sheeted and prepared for their rest. The sepulchre is no longer an empty vault, a dreary charnel, but a chamber of rest, a dormitory furnished and prepared, hung with the arras which Christ Himself has bequeathed. It is now no more a damp, dark, dreary prison: Jesus has changed all that.

> " 'Tis now a cell where angels use
> To come and go with heavenly news."

The angel from heaven rolled away the stone from our Lord's sepulchre and let in the fresh air and light again upon our Lord, and He stepped out more than a conqueror. Death had fled. The grave had capitulated.

> " Lives again our glorious King!
> ' Where, O death, is now thy sting?'
> Once He died our souls to save;
> ' Where's thy victory, boasting grave?' "

Well, brethren, as surely as Christ rose so did He guarantee as an absolute certainty the resurrection of all His saints into a glorious life for their bodies, the life of their souls never having paused even for a moment. In this He conquered death; and since that memorable victory, every day Christ is overcoming death, for He gives His Spirit to His saints, and having that Spirit within them they meet the last enemy without alarm: often they confront Him with songs, perhaps more frequently they face him with calm countenance, and fall asleep with peace. I will not fear thee, death, why should I? Thou lookest like a dragon, but thy sting is gone. Thy teeth are broken, oh old lion, wherefore should I fear thee? I know thou art no more able to destroy me, but thou art sent as a messenger to conduct me to the golden gate wherein I shall enter and see my Saviour's unveiled face for ever. Expiring saints have often said that their last beds have been the best they have ever slept upon. Many of them have enquired,

> " Tell me, my soul, can this be death?"

To die has been so different a thing from what they expected it to be, so lightsome, and so joyous; they have been so unloaded of all care, have felt so relieved instead of burdened, that they have wondered whether this could be the monster they had been so afraid of all their days. They find it a pin's prick, whereas they feared it would prove a sword-thrust: it is the shutting of the eye on earth and the opening of it in heaven, whereas they thought it would have been a stretching upon the rack, or a dreary passage through a dismal region of gloom and dread. Beloved, our exalted Lord has overcome death in all these ways.

But now, observe, that this is not the text:—the text speaks of something yet to be done. The last enemy that *shall be* destroyed is death, so that death in the sense meant by the text is not destroyed yet. He is to be destroyed, and how will that be?

Well, I take it death will be destroyed in the sense first that, at the coming of Christ, *those who are alive and remain shall not see death.* They shall be changed; there must be a change even to the living before they can inherit eternal life, but they shall not actually die. Do not envy them, for they will have no preference beyond those that sleep; rather do I think theirs to be the inferior lot of the two in some respects. But they will not know death: the multitude of the Lord's own who will be alive at His coming will pass into the glory without needing to die. Thus death, as far as they are concerned, will be destroyed.

But the sleeping ones, the myriads who have left their flesh and bones to moulder back to earth, death shall be destroyed even as to them, for when the trumpet sounds they shall rise from the tomb. *The resurrection is the destruction of death.* We never taught, nor believed, nor thought that every particle of every body that was put into the grave would come to its fellow, and that the absolutely identical material would rise; but we do say that the identical body will be raised, and that as surely as there cometh out of the ground the seed that was put into it, though in very different guise, for it cometh not forth as a seed but as a flower, so surely shall the same body rise again. The same material is not necessary, but there shall come out of the grave, ay, come out of the earth, if it never saw a grave, or come out of the sea if devoured by monsters, that selfsame body for true identity which was inhabited by the soul while here below. Was it not so with our Lord? Even so shall it be with His own people, and then shall be brought to pass the saying that is written, "Death is swallowed up in victory. O death, where is thy sting! O grave where is thy victory!"

There will be this feature in our Lord's victory, that death will be fully destroyed because *those who rise will not be one whit the worse for having died.* I believe concerning those new bodies that there will be no trace upon them of the feebleness of old age, none of the marks of long and wearying sickness, none of the scars of martyrdom. Death shall not have left his mark upon them at all, except it be some glory mark which shall be to their honour, like the scars in the flesh of the Well beloved, which are His chief beauty even now in the eyes of those for whom His hands and feet were pierced. In this sense death shall be destroyed because he shall have done no damage to the saints at all, the very trace of decay shall have been swept away from the redeemed.

And then, finally, there shall, after this trumpet of the Lord, be no *more death*, neither sorrow, nor crying, for the former things have passed away. "Christ being raised from the dead dieth no more, death hath no more dominion over him"; and so also the quickened ones, His own redeemed, they too shall die no more. Oh dreadful, dreadful supposition, that they should ever have to undergo temptation or pain, or death a second time. It cannot be. "Because I live," says Christ, "they shall live also." Yet the doctrine of the natural immortality of the soul having been given up by some, certain of them have felt obliged to give up with the eternity of future punishment the eternity of future bliss, and assuredly as far as some great proof texts are concerned, they stand or fall together. "These shall go away into everlasting punishment, and the righteous into life eternal"; if the one state be short so must the other be: whatever the adjective means in the one case it means in the other. To us the word means endless duration in both cases, and we look forward to a bliss which shall never know end or duration. Then in the tearless, sorrowless, graveless country death shall be utterly destroyed.

III. And now last of all, and the word "last" sounds fitly in this case, DEATH IS TO BE DESTROYED LAST. Because he came in last he must go out last. Death was not the first of our foes: first came the devil, then sin, then death. Death is not the worst of enemies; death is an enemy, but he is much to be preferred to our other adversaries. It were better to die a thousand times than to sin. To be tried by death is nothing compared with being tempted by the devil. The mere physical pains connected with dissolution are comparative trifles compared with the hideous grief which is caused by sin and the burden which a sense of guilt causes to the soul. No, death is but a secondary mischief compared with the defilement of sin. Let the great enemies go down first; smite the shepherd and the sheep will be scattered; let sin, and Satan, the lord of all these evils, be smitten first, and death may well be left to the last.

Notice, that death is the last enemy to each individual Christian and the last to be destroyed. Well now, if the word of God says it is the last I want to remind you of a little piece of practical wisdom—leave him to be the last. Brother, do not dispute the appointed order, but let the last be last. I have known a brother wanting to vanquish death long before he died. But, brother, you do not want dying grace till dying moments. What would be the good of dying grace while you are yet alive? A boat will only be needful when you reach a river. Ask for living grace, and glorify Christ thereby, and then you shall have dying grace when dying time comes. Your enemy is going to be destroyed, but not to-day. There is a great host of enemies to be fought to-day, and you may be content to let this one alone for a while. This enemy will be destroyed, but of the times and the seasons we are in ignorance; our wisdom is to be good soldiers of Jesus Christ as the duty of every day requires. Take your trials as they come, brother! God will in due time help you to overcome

I

your last enemy, but meanwhile see to it that you overcome the world, the flesh, and the devil. If you live well you will die well. That same covenant in which the Lord Jesus gave you life contains also the grant of death, for "All things are yours, whether things present or things to come, or life or death, all are yours, and ye are Christ's, and Christ is God's."

Why is death left to the last? Well, I think it is because Christ can make much use of him. The last enemy that shall be destroyed is death, because death is of great service before he is destroyed. Oh, what lessons some of us have learned from death! There are, perhaps, no sermons like the deaths which have happened in our households; the departure of our beloved friends have been to us solemn discourses of divine wisdom, which our heart could not help hearing. So Christ has spared death to make him a preacher to his saints. Brethren, if I may die as I have seen some of our church members die, I court the grand occasion. I would not wish to escape death by some by-road if I may sing as they sang. If I may have such hosannas and hallelujahs beaming in my very eyes as I have seen as well as heard from them, it were a blessed thing to die. Yes, as a supreme test of love and faith, death is well respited awhile to let the saints glorify their Master.

Besides, brethren, without death we should not be so conformed to Christ as we shall be if we fall asleep in Him. If there could be any jealousies in heaven among the saints, I think that any saint who does not die, but is changed when Christ comes, could almost meet me and you, who probably will die, and say, "My brother, there is one thing I have missed, I never lay in the grave, I never had the chill hand of death laid on me, and so in that I was not conformed to my Lord. But *you* know what it is to have fellowship with Him, even in His death." Did I not well say that they that were alive and remain should have no preference over them that are asleep? I think the preference if anything shall belong to us who sleep in Jesus, and wake up in His likeness.

Death, dear friends, is not yet destroyed, because he brings the saints home. He does but come to them and whisper his message, and in a moment they are supremely blessed.

> " Have done with sin and care and woe,
> And with the Saviour rest."

And so death is not destroyed yet, for he answers useful purposes.

But, beloved, he is going to be destroyed. He is the last enemy of the church collectively. The church as a body has had a mass of foes to contend with, but after the resurrection we shall say, "This is the last enemy. Not another foe is left." Eternity shall roll on in ceaseless bliss. There may be changes, bringing new delights; perhaps in the eternity to come there may be eras and ages of yet more amazing bliss, and still more superlative ecstasy; but there shall be

> " No rude alarm of raging foes,
> No cares to break the last repose."

The last enemy that shall be destroyed is death, and if the last be slain there can be no future foe. The battle is fought and the victory is won for ever. And who hath won it? who but the Lamb that sitteth on the throne, to Whom let us all ascribe honour, and glory, and majesty, and power, and dominion, and might, for ever and ever. The Lord help us in our solemn adoration. Amen.

FOLLOWING THE RISEN CHRIST

A Sermon

Text.—"If ye then be risen with Christ, seek those things which are above, where Christ sitteth on the right hand of God. Set your affection on things above, not on things on the earth."—Colossians iii. 1, 2.

THE resurrection of our divine Lord from the dead is the corner-stone of Christian doctrine. Perhaps I might more accurately call it the key-stone of the arch of Christianity, for if that fact could be disproved the whole fabric of the gospel would fall to the ground. If Jesus Christ be not risen then is our preaching vain, and your faith is also vain; ye are yet in your sins. If Christ be not risen, then they which have fallen asleep in Christ have perished, and we ourselves, in missing so glorious a hope as that of resurrection, are of all men the most miserable.

Because of the great importance of His resurrection, our Lord was pleased to give many infallible proofs of it, by appearing again and again in the midst of His followers. It would be interesting to search out how many times He appeared; I think we have mention of some sixteen manifestations. He showed Himself openly before His disciples, and did eat and drink with them. They touched His hands and His side, and heard His voice, and knew that it was the same Jesus that was crucified. He was not content with giving evidence to the ears and to the eyes, but even to the sense of touch He proved the reality of His resurrection.

These appearances were very varied. Sometimes He gave an interview to one alone, either to a man, as to Cephas, or to a woman, as to Magdalene. He conversed with two of His followers as they went to Emmaus, and with the company of the apostles by the sea. We find Him at one moment amongst the eleven when the doors were shut for fear of the Jews, and at another time in the midst of an assembly of more than five hundred brethren, who years after were most of them living witnesses to the fact. They could not all have been deceived. It is not possible that any historical fact could have been placed upon a better basis of credibility than the resurrection of our

Lord from the dead. This is put beyond all dispute and question, and of purpose is it so done, because it is essential to the whole Christian system.

For this same cause the resurrection of Christ is commemorated frequently. There is no ordinance in Scripture of any one Lord's-day in the year being set apart to commemorate the rising of Christ from the dead, for this reason, that every Lord's-day is the memorial of our Lord's resurrection. Wake up any Lord's-day you please, whether in the depth of winter, or in the warmth of summer, and you may sing:—

> " To-day He rose and left the dead,
>   And Satan's empire fell;
> To-day the saints His triumph spread,
>   And all His wonders tell."

To set apart an Easter Sunday for special memory of the resurrection is a human device, for which there is no Scriptural command, but to make every Lord's-day an Easter Sunday is due to Him Who rose early on the first day of the week. We gather together on the first rather than upon the seventh day of the week, because redemption is even a greater work than creation, and more worthy of commemoration, and because the rest which followed creation is far outdone by that which ensues upon the completion of redemption. Like the apostles, we meet on the first day of the week, and hope that Jesus may stand in our midst, and say, "Peace be unto you." Our Lord has lifted the Sabbath from the old and rusted hinges whereon the law had placed it long before, and set it on the new golden hinges which His love has fashioned. He hath placed our rest-day, not at the end of a week of toil, but at the beginning of the rest which remaineth for the people of God. Every first day of the week we should meditate upon the rising of our Lord, and seek to enter into fellowship with Him in His risen life.

Never let us forget that all who are in Him rose from the dead in His rising. Next in importance to the fact of the resurrection is the doctrine of the federal headship of Christ, and the unity of all His people with Him. It is because we are in Christ that we become partakers of everything that Christ did—we are circumcised with Him, dead with Him, buried with Him, risen with Him, because we cannot be separated from Him. We are members of His body, and not a bone of Him can be broken. Because that union is most intimate, continuous, and indissoluble, therefore all that concerns Him concerns us, and as He rose so all His people have arisen in Him.

They are risen in two ways. First, representatively. All the elect rose in Christ in the day when He quitted the tomb. He was justified, or declared to be clear of all liabilities on account of our sins, by being set free from the prison-house of the tomb. There was no reason for detaining Him in the sepulchre, for He had discharged the debts of His people by dying "unto sin once." He was our hostage and our representative, and when He came forth from His bonds we came forth in Him. We have endured the sentence of the law in our Substitute, we have lain in its prison, and even died under its death-warrant, and now we are no longer under its curse. "Now if we be dead with Christ, we believe that we shall also live with him: knowing that Christ being raised from the dead dieth no more; death hath no more dominion over him. For in that he died, he died unto sin once; but in that he liveth, he liveth unto God."

Next to this representative resurrection comes our spiritual resurrection, which is ours as soon as we are led by faith to believe in Jesus Christ. Then it may be said of us, "And you hath he quickened who were dead in trespasses and sins."

The resurrection blessing is to be perfected by-and-by at the appearing of our Lord and Saviour, for then our bodies shall rise again, if we fall asleep before His coming. He redeemed our manhood in its entirety, spirit, soul, and body, and He will not be content until the resurrection which has passed upon our spirit shall pass upon our body too. These dry bones shall live; together with His dead body they shall rise.

> "When He arose ascending high,
>   He showed our feet the way;
> Up to the Lord our flesh shall fly
>   At the great rising day."

Then shall we know in the perfection of our resurrection beauty that we are indeed completely risen in Christ, and "as in Adam all die, so in Christ shall all be made alive."

This morning we shall only speak of our fellowship with Christ in His resurrection as to our own spiritual resurrection. Do not misunderstand me as if I thought the resurrection to be only spiritual, for a literal rising from the dead is yet to come; but our text speaks of spiritual resurrection, and I shall therefore endeavour to set it before you.

I. First, then, LET US CONSIDER OUR SPIRITUAL RISING WITH CHRIST: "If ye then be risen with Christ." Though the words look like a supposition they are not meant to be so. The apostle casts no doubt, and raises no question, but merely puts it thus for argument's sake. It might just as well be read, "Since ye then are risen in Christ." The "if" is used logically, not theologically: by way of argument, and not by way of doubt. All who believe in Christ are risen with Christ. Let us meditate on this truth.

For, first, we were "dead in trespasses and sins," but having believed in Christ *we have been quickened by the Holy Ghost,* and we are dead no longer. There we lay in the tomb, ready to become corrupt. We lay in our death quite unable to raise ourselves therefrom; ours were eyes that could not see, and ears that could not hear; a heart that could not love; and a withered hand that could not be stretched out to give the touch of faith. We were as guilty as if we had power, for the loss of moral power is not the loss of moral responsibility: we were, therefore, in a state of spiritual death of the most fearful kind. The Holy Spirit visited us and made us live.

We remember the first sensation of life, some of us—how it seemed to tingle in our soul's veins with pain sharp and bitter; just as drowning persons when life is coming back to them suffer great pain; so did we. Conviction was wrought in us and confession of sin, a dread of judgment to come and a sense of present condemnation; but these were tokens of life, and that life gradually deepened and opened up until the eye was opened—we could see Christ, the hand ceased to be withered, and we stretched it out and touched His garment's hem; the feet began to move in the way of obedience, and the heart felt the sweet glow of love within. Then the eyes, not content with seeing, fell to weeping; and afterwards, when the tears were wiped away, they flashed and sparkled with delight.

Oh, my brethren, believers in Jesus, you are not spiritually dead any longer; on Christ you have believed, and that grand act proves that you are no more dead. You have been quickened by God according to the working of His mighty power, which He wrought in Christ when He raised Him from the dead, and set Him at His own right hand in the heavenlies. Now, beloved, you are new creatures, the produce of a second birth, begotten again in Christ Jesus unto newness of life. Christ is your life; such a life as you never knew before, nor could have known apart from Him. If ye then be risen with Christ ye walk in newness of life, while the world abideth in death.

Let us advance another step: we are risen with Christ, and therefore *there has been wrought in us a wonderful change.* When the dead shall rise they will not appear as they now are. The buried seed rises from the ground, but not as a seed, for it puts forth green leaf, and bud, and stem, and gradually developes expanding flower and fruit, and even so we wear a new form, for we are renewed after the image of Him that created us in righteousness and holiness.

I ask you to consider the change which the Spirit of God has

wrought in the believer: a wonderful change indeed! Before
regeneration our soul was as our body will be when it dies;
and we read that "it is sown in corruption." There was corruption in our mind and it was working irresistibly towards
every evil and offensive thing. In many the corruption did not
appear upon the surface, but it worked within; in others it was
conspicuous and fearful to look upon. How great the change!
For now the power of corruption within us is broken, the new
life has overcome it, for it is a living and incorruptible seed
which liveth and abideth for ever. Corruption is upon the old
nature, but it cannot touch the new, which is our true and real
self. Is it not a great thing to be purged of the filthiness which
would have ultimately brought us down to Tophet where the
fire unquenchable burns, and the worm undying feeds upon
the corrupt?

When a body is buried, we are told by the apostle again that
it is "sown in weakness." The poor dead frame cannot lay
itself down in its last bed, friendly hands must place it there;
even so we were utter weakness towards all good. When we
were the captives of sin we could do nothing good, even as our
Lord said, "Without me ye can do nothing." We were incapable
of even a good thought apart from Him. But "when we were
yet without strength, in due time Christ died for the ungodly";
and now we know Him and the power of His resurrection. God
hath given us the spirit of power and of love; is it not written,
"As many as received him, to them gave he power to become
the sons of God, even to them that believe on his name"? This
change from the natural to the spiritual is such as only God
Himself could have wrought, and yet we have experienced it.
To God be the glory. So that by virtue of our rising in Christ
we have received life and have become the subjects of a wondrous
change—"old things are passed away; behold, all things are
become new."

In consequence of our receiving this life and undergoing this
change *the things of the world and sin become a tomb to us*. To a
dead man a sepulchre is as good a dwelling as he can want. You
may call it his bedchamber, if you will; for he lies within it
as unconscious as if he were in slumber. But the moment the
dead man lives, he will not endure such a bedchamber; he calls
it a dreary vault, a loathsome dungeon, an unbearable charnel,
and he must leave it at once. So when you and I were natural
men, and had no spiritual life, the things of this life contented
us; but it is far otherwise now. A merely outward religion was
all that we desired; a dead form suited a dead soul. Judaism
pleased those who were under its yoke, in the very beginning
of the gospel; new moons and holy days and traditional

ordinances, and fasting and feasting were great things with those who forgot their resurrection with Christ. All those things make pretty furniture for a dead man's chamber; but when the eternal life enters the soul these outward ordinances are flung off, the living man rends off his grave clothes, tears away his cerements, and demands such garments as are suitable for life. So the apostle in the chapter before our text tells us to let no man spoil us by the traditions of men and the inventions of a dead ritualism, for these things are not the portion of renewed and spiritual men.

So, too, all merely carnal objects become as a grave to us, whether they be sinful pleasures or selfish gains. For the dead man the shroud, the coffin, and the vault are suitable enough; but make the corpse alive again, and he cannot rest in the coffin; he makes desperate struggles to break it up. See how by main force he dashes up the lid, rends off his bandages, and leaps from the bier. So the man renewed by grace cannot abide sin, it is a coffin to him: he cannot bear evil pleasures, they are as a shroud; he cries for liberty. When resurrection comes the man uplifts the hillock above his grave, and scatters monument and head-stone, if these are raised above him. Some souls are buried under a mass of self-righteousness, like wealthy men on whom shrines of marble have been heaped; but all these the believer shakes off, he must have them away, he cannot bear these dead works. He cannot live otherwise than by faith; all other life is death to him. He must get out of his former state; for as a tomb is not a fit place for a living man, so when we are quickened by grace the things of sin, and self, and carnal sense become dreary catacombs to us, wherein our soul feels buried, and out of which we must arise. How can we that are raised out of the death of sin live any longer therein?

And, now, beloved, *we are at this time wholly raised from the dead* in a spiritual sense. Let us think of this, for our Lord did not have His head quickened while His feet remained in the sepulchre; but He rose a perfect and entire Man, alive throughout. Even so have we been renewed in every part. We have received, though it be but in its infancy, a perfect spiritual life: we are perfect in Christ Jesus. In our inner man our eye is opened, our ear is awakened, our hand is active, our foot is nimble: our every faculty is there, though as yet immature, and needing development, and having the old dead nature to contend with.

Moreover, and best of all, we are so raised that *we shall die no more*. Oh, tell me no more the dreary tale that a man who has received the divine life may yet lose grace and perish. With our Bibles in our hands we know better. "Christ being raised from the dead dieth no more, death hath no more dominion over him," and therefore he that hath received Christ's life in him shall never die. Hath He not said, "He that believeth in me, though he were dead yet shall he live; and whosoever liveth and believeth in me shall never die"? This life which He has given us shall be in us "a well of water, springing up unto everlasting life." He has Himself said, "I give unto my sheep eternal life, and they shall never perish, neither shall any pluck them out of my hand." On the day of our quickening we bid farewell to spiritual death, and to the sepulchre wherein we slept under sin's dominion. Farewell, thou deadly love of sin; we have done with thee! Farewell, dead world, corrupt world; we have done with thee! Christ has raised us. Christ has given us eternal life. We forsake for ever the dreary abodes of death, and seek the heavenly places. Our Jesus lives, and because He lives we shall live also, world without end.

Thus I have tried to work out the metaphor of resurrection, by which our spiritual renewal is so well set forth.

II. We are urged by the apostle to use the life which we have received, and so, secondly, LET US EXERCISE THE NEW LIFE IN SUITABLE PURSUITS. "If ye then be risen with Christ, seek those things which are above." Let your actions be agreeable to your new life.

First, then, *let us leave the sepulchre.* If we are quickened, our first act should be to leave the region of death. Let us quit the vault of a merely outward religion, and let us worship God in spirit and in truth. Let us have done with priestcraft, and all the black business of spiritual undertaking, and let the dead bury their dead; we will have none of it. Let us have done with outward forms, and rites, and ceremonies, which are not of Christ's ordaining, and let us know nothing save Christ crucified; for that which is not of the living Lord is a mere piece of funeral pomp, fit for the cemeteries of formalists, whose whole religion is a shovelling in of dust on coffin-lids. "Earth to earth, ashes to ashes, dust to dust." "That which is born of the flesh is flesh."

Let us also quit the vault of carnal enjoyments, wherein men seek to satisfy themselves with provision for the flesh. Let us not live by the sight of the eye, nor by the hearing of the ear. Let us not live for the amassing of wealth, or the gaining of fame, for these ought to be as dead things to the man who is risen in Christ. Let us not live for the world which we see, nor after the fashion of men to whom this life is everything. Let us live as those that have come out of the world, and who, though they are in it, are no more of it. Let us be unmindful of the country from whence we came out, and leave it, as Abraham did, as though there were no such country, henceforth dwelling with our God, sojourners with Him, seeking "a city which hath foundations, whose builder and maker is God." As Jesus Christ left behind Him all the abodes of death, let us do the same.

And, then, let us *hasten to forget every evil, even as our Lord hastened to leave the tomb.* How little a time, after all, did He sojourn among the dead. He must needs lie in the heart of the earth three days, but He made them as short as possible, so that it is difficult to make out the three days at all. They were there, for there were fragments of each period, but surely never were three days so short as Jesus made them. He cut them short in righteousness, and being loosed from the pains of death, He rose early, at the very break of day. At the first instant that it was possible for Him to get away from the sepulchre consistently with the Scriptures He left the napkin and the grave-clothes, and stood in the garden, waiting to salute His disciples. So let it be with us: there should be no lingering, no loitering, no hankering after the world, no clinging to its vanities, no making provision for the flesh. Up in the morning early, oh ye who are spiritually quickened! Up in the morning early, from your ease, your carnal pleasure, your love of wealth and self, and away out from the dark vault into a congenial sphere of action: "If ye then be risen with Christ, seek those things which are above."

To pursue the analogy: when our Lord had left the tomb thus early He spent a season on earth among His disciples, *and we are to pass the time of our sojourning here on earth, as His was passed, and in holy service.* Our Lord reckoned that He was on the move from earth as soon as He rose. If you remember, He said, "I ascend unto my Father, and your Father." He did not say, "I shall ascend," as though He looked at it as a future thing; but He said, "I ascend," as if it were so quickly to be done that it was already doing. Forty days He stayed, for He had forty days' work to do; but He looked upon Himself as already going up into heaven. He had done with the world, He had done with the grave, and now He said, "I ascend to my Father, and your Father."

We also have our forty days to tarry here; the period may be longer or shorter as the providence of God ordains, but it will soon be over, and the time of our departure will come. Let us spend our risen life on earth as Jesus spent His,—in a greater seclusion from the world and in greater nearness to heaven than ever. Our Lord occupied Himself much in testimony, manifesting Himself, as we have already seen, in divers ways, to His friends and followers. Let us also manifest the fruits of our risen life, and bear testimony to the power of God. Let all men see that you are risen. So live that there can be no more doubt about your spiritual resurrection than there was about Christ's literal resurrection. Let us spend the time of our sojourning here in the fear of God worshipping Him, serving Him, glorifying Him, endeavouring to set everything in order for the extension of our Master's kingdom, for the comforting of His saints, for the accomplishment of His sacred purposes.

But now I have led you up so far, I want to go further and rise higher. May the Lord help us. *Let our minds ascend to heaven in Christ.* Even while our bodies are here we are to be drawn upwards with Christ; attracted to Him, so that we can say, "He hath raised us up together and made us sit together in heavenly places in Christ Jesus." Our text saith, "Seek those things which are above where Christ sitteth on the right hand of God"; what is this but rising to heavenly pursuits? Jesus has gone up; let us go up with Him. As to these bodies, we cannot as yet ascend, for they are not fit to inherit the kingdom of God; yet let our thoughts and hearts mount up and build a happy rest on high. Let not a stray thought alone ascend like one lone bird which sings and mounts the sky; but let our whole mind, soul, spirit, heart, arise as when doves fly as a cloud.

Let us be practical, too, and in very deed seek the things that are above: seek them because we feel we need them; seek them because we greatly prize them; seek them because we hope to gain them; for a man will not heartily seek for that which he hath no hope of obtaining. The things which are above which we are even now to seek are such as these; let us seek heavenly communion, for we are no more numbered with the congregation of the dead, but we have fellowship in Christ's resurrection, and with all the risen ones. "Truly our fellowship is with the Father and with his Son Jesus Christ," and "our conversation is in heaven." Let us seek to walk with the living God, and to know the fellowship of the Spirit.

Let us seek heavenly graces; for "every good gift and every perfect gift is from above." Let us seek more faith, more love, more patience, more zeal: let us labour after greater charity, greater brotherly kindness, greater humbleness of spirit. Let us labour after likeness to Christ, that He may be the firstborn among many brethren. Seek to bear the image of the heavenly, and to wear those jewels which adorn heavenly spirits.

"Seek those things which are above," that is, heavenly joys. Oh seek to know on earth the peace of heaven, the rest of heaven, the victory of heaven, the service of heaven, the communion of heaven, the holiness of heaven: you may have foretastes of all these; seek after them. Seek, in a word, to be preparing for the heaven which Christ is preparing for you. You are soon to dwell above; robe yourselves for the great festival. Your treasure is above, let your hearts be with it. All that you are to possess in eternity is above, where Christ is; rise, then, and enjoy it. Let hope anticipate the joys which are reserved, and so let us begin our heaven here below. If ye then be risen with Christ, live according to your risen nature, for your life is hid with Christ in God.

What a magnet to draw us towards heaven should this fact be,—that Christ sitteth at God's right hand. Where should the wife's thoughts be when her husband is away but with the absent and beloved one? You know, brethren, it is not otherwise with us: the objects of our affection are always followed by our thoughts. Let Jesus, then, be as a great loadstone, drawing our meditations and affections towards Himself. He is *sitting*, for His work is done; as it is written, "This man, when he had offered one sacrifice for sins for ever, sat down at the right hand of God." Let us rise and rest with Him. He is sitting on a throne. Observe His majesty, delight in His power, and trust in His dominion. He is sitting at the right hand of God in the place of honour and favour. This is a proof that we are beloved and favoured of God, for our representative has the choicest place, at God's right hand. Let your hearts ascend and enjoy that love and favour with Him. Take wing, my thoughts, and fly away to Jesus. My soul, hast thou not often said, "Woe's me that I dwell in Meshech, and tabernacle in the tents of Kedar: oh that I had wings like a dove, that I might flee away and be at rest"? Now, then, my soul, here are wings for thee. Jesus draws thee upward. Thou hast a right to be where Jesus is, for thou art married to Him; therefore let thy thoughts abide with Him, rest in Him, delight in Him, rejoice in Him, and yet again rejoice. The sacred ladder is before us; let us climb it until by faith we sit in the heavenlies with Him.

May the Spirit of God bless these words to you.

III. Thirdly, inasmuch as we are risen with Christ, LET THE NEW LIFE DELIGHT ITSELF IN SUITABLE OBJECTS. This brings in the second verse: "Set your affection on things above, not on things on the earth." "Set your affection." These words do not quite express the meaning, though they are as near it as any one clause could well come. We might render it thus: "Have a relish for things above"; or, "study industriously things above"; or, "set your mind on things above, not on things on the earth." That which is proper enough for a dead man is quite unsuitable for a risen one. Objects of desire which might suit us when we were sinners are not legitimate nor worthy objects for us when we are made saints. As we are quickened we must exercise life, and as we have ascended we must love higher things than those of earth.

What are these "things above" which we should set our affection upon? I ask you now to lift your eyes above yon clouds and this lower firmament to the residence of God. What see you there? First, there is *God Himself*. Make Him the subject of your thoughts, your desires, your emotions, your love. "Delight thyself also in the Lord, and he will give thee the desires of thine heart." "My soul, wait thou only upon God, for my expectation is from him." Call Him "God my exceeding joy." Let nothing come between you and your heavenly Father. What is all the world if you have not God, and when you once have God, what matters it though all the world be gone? God is all things, and when thou canst say "God is mine," thou art richer than Crœsus. O to say, "Whom have I in heaven but thee? and there is none upon earth that I desire beside thee." O to love God with all our heart, and with all our soul, and with all our mind, and with all our strength: that is what the law required, it is what the gospel enables us to render.

What see I next? I see *Jesus*, who is God, but yet is truly Man. Need I press upon you, beloved, to set your love upon the Well-beloved? Has He not won your heart, and doth He not hold it now as under a mighty spell? I know you love Him. Fix your mind on Him then. Often meditate upon His divine person, His perfect work, His mediatorial glory, His second coming, His glorious reign, His love for you, your own security in Him, your union with Him. Oh let these sweet thoughts possess your breasts, fill your mouths, and influence your lives. Let the morning break with thoughts of Christ, and let your last thought at night be sweetened with His presence. Set your affection upon Him Who has set His affection upon you.

But what next do I see above? I see *the new Jerusalem*, which is the mother of us all. I see the church of Christ triumphant in heaven, with which the church militant is one. We do not often enough realize the fact that we are come unto the general assembly and church of the firstborn, whose names are written in heaven. Love all the saints, but do not forget the saints above. Have fellowship with them, for we make but one communion. Remember those:—

> " Who once were mourning here below,
>   And wet their couch with tears,
> Who wrestled hard, as we do now,
>   With sins, and doubts, and fears."

Speak with the braves who have won their crowns, the heroes who have fought a good fight, and now rest from their labours, waving the palm. Let your hearts be often among the perfected, with whom you are to spend eternity.

And what else is there above that our hearts should love but *heaven itself?* It is the place of holiness; let us so love it that we begin to be holy here. It is the place of rest; let us so delight in it that by faith we enter into that rest. O my brethren, you have vast estates which you have never seen; and methinks if I had an estate on earth which was soon to be mine I should wish to take a peep over the hedge now and then. If I could not take possession, I should like to see what I had in reversion. I would make an excuse to pass that way and say to any who were with me, "That estate is going to be mine before long." In your present poverty console yourselves with the many mansions. In your sickness delight much in the land where the inhabitants shall no more say, "I am sick." In the midst of depression of spirit comfort your heart with the prospect of unmixed felicity.

> " No more fatigue, no more distress,
> Nor sin nor death shall reach the place;
> No groans to mingle with the songs
> Which warble from immortal tongues."

What! Are you fettered to earth? Can you not project yourself into the future? The stream of death is narrow; cannot your imagination and your faith leap over the brook to stand on the hither shore awhile and cry, "All is mine, and mine for ever. Where Jesus is there shall I be; where Jesus sits there shall I rest:

> " Far from a world of grief and sin,
> With God eternally shut in ? "

"Set your affection on things above." Oh to get away at this present time from these dull cares which like a fog envelope us! Even we that are Christ's servants, and live in His court, at times feel weary, and droop as if His service were hard. He never means it to be a bondage, and it is our fault if we make it so. Martha's service is due, but she is not called to be *cumbered* with much serving; that is her own arrangement: let us serve abundantly, and yet sit with Mary at the Master's feet.

You who are in business, and mix with the world by the necessity of your callings, must find it difficult to keep quite clear of the down-dragging influences of this poor world; it will hamper you if it can. You are like a bird, which is always in danger when it alights on the earth. There are lime-twigs, and traps, and nets, and guns, and a poor bird is never safe except upon the wing and up aloft. Yet birds must come down to feed, and they do well to gather their meal in haste, and take to their wings again. When we come down among men we must speedily be up again. When you have to mix with the world, and see its sin and evil, yet take heed that you do not light on the ground without your Father: and then, as soon as ever you have picked up your barley, rise again, away, away, for this is not your rest. You are like Noah's dove flying over the waste of waters, there is no rest for the sole of your feet but on the ark with Jesus.

On this resurrection-day fence out the world, let us chase away the wild boar of the wood, and let the vines bloom, and the tender grapes give forth their good smell, and let the Beloved come and walk in the garden of our souls, while we delight ourselves in Him and in His heavenly gifts. Let us not carry our burden of things below on this holy day, but let us keep it as a Sabbath unto the Lord. On the Sabbath we are no more to work with our minds than with our hands. Cares and anxieties of an earthly kind defile the day of sacred rest. The essence of Sabbath-breaking lies in worry, and murmuring, and unbelief, with which too many are filled. Put these away, beloved, for we are risen with Christ, and it is not meet that we should wander among the tombs. Nay, rather let us sing unto the Lord a new song, and praise Him with our whole soul.

THE RESURRECTION OF OUR LORD JESUS

A Sermon

Text.—"Remember that Jesus Christ of the seed of David was raised from the dead according to my gospel."—2 Timothy ii. 8.

Our text is found in Paul's second letter to Timothy. The venerable minister is anxious about the young man who has preached with remarkable success, and whom he regards in some respects as his successor. The old man is about to put off his tabernacle, and he is concerned that his son in the gospel, should preach the same truth as his father has preached, and should by no means adulterate the gospel. A tendency showed itself in Timothy's day, and the same tendency exists at this very hour, to try to get away from the simple matters of fact upon which our religion is built, to something more philosophical and hard to be understood. The word which the common people heard gladly is not fine enough for cultured sages, and so they must needs surround it with a mist of human thought and speculation.

Three or four plain facts constitute the gospel, even as Paul puts it in the fifteenth chapter of his first Epistle to the Corinthians: "For I delivered unto you first of all that which I also received, how that Christ died for our sins according to the Scriptures; and that he was buried, and that he rose again the third day according to the Scriptures." Upon the incarnation, life, death, and resurrection of Jesus our salvation hinges. He who believes these truths aright hath believed the gospel, and believing the gospel he shall without doubt find eternal salvation therein.

But men want novelties; they cannot endure that the trumpet should give forth the same certain sound, they crave some fresh fantasia every day. "*The gospel with variations*" is the music for them. Intellect is progressive, they say; they must, therefore, march ahead of their forefathers. Incarnate Deity, a holy life, an atoning death, and a literal resurrection,—having heard these things now for nearly nineteen centuries they are just a little stale, and the cultivated mind hungers for a change from the old-fashioned manna. Even in Paul's day this tendency was manifest, and so they sought to regard facts as mysteries or parables, and they laboured to find a spiritual meaning in them

till they went so far as to deny them as actual facts. The Apostle
Paul was very anxious that Timothy at least should stand firm
to the old witness, and should understand in their plain meaning
his testimonies to the fact that Jesus Christ of the seed of David
rose again from the dead.

Within the compass of this verse several facts are recorded:
and, first, there is here the great truth that Jesus, the Son of
the Highest, was anointed of God; the apostle calls Him "Jesus
Christ," that is, the anointed One, the Messiah, the sent of God.
He calls Him also "*Jesus*," which signifies a Saviour, and it
is a grand truth that He Who was born of Mary, He Who was
laid in the manger at Bethlehem, He Who loved and lived and
died for us, is the ordained and anointed Saviour of men. We
have not a moment's doubt about the mission, office, and design
of our Lord Jesus; in fact, we hang our soul's salvation upon
His being anointed of the Lord to be the Saviour of men.

This Jesus Christ was really and truly man; for Paul says He
was "*of the seed of David*." True He was divine, and His birth
was not after the ordinary manner of men, but still He was in
all respects partaker of our human nature, and came of the
stock of David. This also we do believe. We are not among
those who spiritualize the incarnation, and suppose that God
was here as a phantom, or that the whole story is but an instructive legend. Nay, in very flesh and blood did the Son of God
abide among men: bone of our bone and flesh of our flesh:
was He in the days of His sojourn here below. We know and
believe that Jesus Christ has come in the flesh. We love the
incarnate God and in Him we fix our trust.

It is implied, too, in the text that *Jesus died;* for He could
not be raised from the dead if He had not first gone down among
the dead, and been one of them. Yes, Jesus died: the crucifixion
was no delusion, the piercing of His side with a spear was most
clear and evident proof that He was dead: His heart was pierced,
and the blood and water flowed therefrom. As a dead man
He was taken down from the cross and carried by gentle hands,
and laid in Joseph's virgin tomb. I think I see that pale corpse,
white as a lily. Mark how it is distained with the blood of His
five wounds, which make Him red as the rose. See how the
holy women tenderly wrap Him in fine linen with sweet spices,
and leave Him to spend His Sabbath all alone in the rock-hewn
sepulchre. No man in this world was ever more surely dead
than He. "He made his grave with the wicked and with the
rich in his death." As dead they laid Him in the place of the
dead, with napkin and grave-clothes, and habiliments fit for a
grave: then they rolled the great stone at the grave's mouth
and left Him, knowing that He was dead.

Then comes the grand truth, that as soon as ever the third sun commenced his shining circuit *Jesus rose again*. His body had not decayed, for it was not possible for that holy thing to see corruption; but still it had been dead; and by the power of God—by His own power, by the Father's power, by the power of the Spirit—for it is attributed to each of these in turn, before the sun had risen His dead body was quickened. The silent heart began again to beat, and through the stagnant canals of the veins the life-flood began to circulate. The soul of the Redeemer again took possession of the body, and it lived once more. There He was within the sepulchre, as truly living as to all parts of Him as He had ever been. He literally and truly, in a material body, came forth from the tomb to live among men till the hour of His ascension into heaven. This is the truth which is still to be taught, refine it who may, spiritualize it who dare. This is the historical fact which the apostles witnessed; this is the truth for which the confessors bled and died. This is the doctrine which is the key-stone of the arch of Christianity, and they that hold it not have cast aside the essential truth of God. How can they hope for salvation for their souls if they do not believe that "the Lord is risen indeed"?

This morning I wish to do three things. First, let us *consider the bearings of the resurrection of Christ upon other great truths ;* secondly, let us consider *the bearings of this fact upon the gospel,* for it has such bearings, according to the text—"Jesus Christ of the seed of David was raised from the dead according to my gospel"; thirdly, let us *consider its bearings on ourselves,* which are all indicated in the word "Remember."

I. First, then, beloved, as God shall help us, let us CONSIDER THE BEARINGS OF THE FACT THAT JESUS ROSE FROM THE DEAD.

It is clear at the outset that *the resurrection of our Lord was a tangible proof that there is another life.* Have you not quoted a great many times certain lines about "That undiscovered country from whose bourne no traveller returns"? It is not so. There was once a traveller who said that "I go to prepare a place for you, and if I go away I will come again and receive you unto myself; that where I am there ye may be also." He said, "A little time and ye shall see me, and again a little time and ye shall not see me, and because I go to the Father." Do you not remember these words of His? Our divine Lord went to the undiscovered country, and He returned. He said that at the third day He would be back again, and He was true to his word.

There is no doubt that there is another state for human life, for Jesus has been in it, and has come back from it. We have no doubt as to a future existence, for Jesus existed after death.

We have no doubt as to a paradise of future bliss, for Jesus went to it and returned. Though He has left us again, yet that coming back to tarry with us forty days has given us a sure pledge that He will return a second time when the hour is due, and then will be with us for a thousand years, and reign on earth amongst His ancients gloriously. His return from among the dead is a pledge to us of existence after death, and we rejoice in it.

His resurrection is also a pledge that the body will surely live again and rise to a superior condition; for the body of our blessed Master was no phantom after death any more than before. "Handle me, and see." Oh wondrous proof! He said, "Handle me, and see"; and then to Thomas, "Reach hither thy finger, and behold my hands; and reach hither thy hand, and thrust it into my side." What deception is possible here? The risen Jesus was no mere spirit. He promptly cried, "A spirit hath not flesh and bones, as ye see me have." "Bring me," said He, "something to eat"; and as if to show how real His body was, though He did not need to eat, yet He did eat, and a piece of a broiled fish and of an honeycomb were proofs of the reality of the act.

Now, the body of our Lord in its risen state did not exhibit the whole of His glorification, for otherwise we should have seen John falling at His feet as dead, and we should have seen all His disciples overcome with the glory of the vision; but, still, in a great measure, we may call the forty days' sojourn— "The life of Jesus in his glory upon earth." He was no longer despised and rejected of men; but a glory surrounded Him. It is evident that the raised body passed from place to place in a single moment, that it appeared and vanished at will, and was superior to the laws of matter. The risen body was incapable of pain, of hunger, thirst, and weariness during the time in which it remained here below,—fit representative of the bulk of which it was the firstfruits. Of our body also it shall be said ere long, "It was sown in weakness, it is raised in power: it was sown in dishonour, it is raised in glory."

Secondly, *Christ's rising from the dead was the seal to all His claims.* It was true, then, that He was sent of God, for God raised Him from the dead in confirmation of His mission. He had said Himself, "Destroy this body, and in three days I will raise it up." Lo, there He is: the temple of His body is rebuilt! He had even given this as a sign, that as Jonas was three days and three nights in the whale's belly, so should the Son of man be three days and three nights in the heart of the earth, and should then come forth to life again. Behold His own appointed sign fulfilled! Before men's eye the seal is manifest! Suppose He had never risen. You and I might have believed in the truth of a certain mission which God had given Him; but we could never have believed in the truth of such a commission as He claimed to have received—a commission to be our Redeemer from death and hell. How could He be our ransom from the grave if He had Himself remained under the dominion of death?

Dear friends, the rising of Christ from the dead proved that this man was innocent of every sin. He could not be holden by the bands of death, for there was no sin to make those bands fast. Corruption could not touch His pure body, for no original sin had defiled the Holy One. Death could not keep Him a continual prisoner, because He had not actually come under sin; and though He took sin of ours, and bore it by imputation, and therefore died, yet He had no fault of His own, and must, therefore, be set free when His imputed load had been removed.

Moreover, Christ's rising from the dead proved His claim to Deity. We are told in another place that He was proved to be the Son of God with power by the resurrection from the dead. He raised Himself by His own power, and though the Father and the Holy Spirit were co-operative with Him, and hence His resurrection is ascribed to them, yet it was because the Father had given Him to have life in Himself, that therefore He arose from the dead. Oh, risen Saviour, Thy rising is the seal of Thy work! We can have no doubt about Thee now that Thou hast left the tomb. Prophet of Nazareth, Thou art indeed the Christ of God, for God has loosed the bands of death for Thee! Son of David, Thou art indeed the elect and precious One, for Thou ever livest! Thy resurrection life has set the sign-manual of heaven to all that Thou hast said and done, and for this we bless and magnify Thy name.

A third bearing of his resurrection is this, and it is a very grand one,—*The resurrection of our Lord, according to Scripture, was the acceptance of His sacrifice.* By the Lord Jesus Christ rising from the dead evidence was given that He had fully endured the penalty which was due to human guilt. "The soul that sinneth it shall die"—that is the determination of the God of heaven. Jesus stands in the sinner's stead and dies: and when He has done *that* nothing more can be demanded of Him, for He that is dead is free from the law. You take a man who has been guilty of a capital offence: he is condemned to be hanged, he is hanged by the neck till he is dead—what more has the law to do with him? It has done with him, for it has executed its sentence upon him; if he can be brought back to life again he is clear from the law; no writ that runs in Her Majesty's dominions can touch him—he has suffered the penalty.

So when our Lord Jesus rose from the dead, after having died, He had fully paid the penalty that was due to justice for the sin of His people, and His new life was a life clear of penalty, free from liability. You and I are clear from the claims of the law because Jesus stood in our stead, and God will not exact payment both from us and from our Substitute: it were contrary to justice to sue both the Surety and those for whom He stood. And now, joy upon joy! the burden of liability which once did lie upon the Substitute is removed from Him also; seeing He has by the suffering of death vindicated justice and made satisfaction to the injured law. Now both the sinner and the Surety are free. This is a great joy, a joy for which to make the golden harps ring out a loftier style of music. He who took our debt has now delivered Himself from it by dying on the cross. His new life, now that He has risen from the dead, is a life free from legal claim, and it is the token to us that we whom He represented are free also.

Listen! "Who shall lay anything to the charge of God's elect? It is God that justifieth, who is he that condemneth? It is Christ that died, yea rather, that is risen again." It is a knock-down blow to fear when the apostle says that we cannot be condemned because Christ has died in our stead, but he puts a double force into it when he cries, "Yea rather, that is risen again." If Satan, therefore, shall come to any believer and say, "What about your sin?" tell him Jesus died for it, and your sin is put away. If he come a second time, and say to you, "What about your sin?" answer him, "Jesus lives, and His life is the assurance of our justification; for if our Surety had not paid the debt He would still be under the power of death." Inasmuch as Jesus has discharged all our liabilities, and left not one farthing due to God's justice from one of His people, He lives and is clear, and we live in Him, and are clear also by virtue of our union with Him. Is not this a glorious doctrine, this doctrine of the resurrection, in its bearing upon the justification of the saints? The Lord Jesus gave Himself for our sins, but He rose again for our justification.

Bear with me while I notice, next, another bearing of this resurrection of Christ. *It was a guarantee of His people's resurrection.* There is a great truth that never is to be forgotten, namely, that Christ and His people are one just as Adam and all his seed are one. That which Adam did He did as a head for a body, and as our Lord Jesus and all believers are one, so that which Jesus did He did as a head for a body. We were crucified together with Christ, we were buried with Christ, and we are risen together with Him; yea, He hath raised us up together and made us sit together in the heavenly places in Christ Jesus. He says, "Because I live ye shall live also." If Christ be not raised from the dead your faith is vain, and our preaching is vain, and ye are yet in your sins, and those that have fallen asleep in Christ have perished, and you will perish too; but if Christ has been raised from the dead then all His people must be raised also; it is a matter of gospel necessity. There is no logic more imperative than the argument drawn from union with Christ. God has made the saints one with Christ, and if Christ has risen all the saints must rise too. My soul takes firm hold on this and as she strengthens her grasp she loses all fear of death. Now we bear our dear ones to the cemetery and leave them each one in his narrow cell, calmly bidding him farewell and saying—

> " So Jesus slept: God's dying Son
> Pass'd through the grave, and blest the bed;
> Rest here, dear saint, till from His throne
> The morning break, and pierce the shade."

It is not merely ours to know that our brethren are living in heaven, but also that their mortal parts are in divine custody, securely kept till the appointed hour when the body shall be reanimated, and the perfect man shall enjoy the adoption of God. We are sure that our dead men shall live; together with Christ's dead body they shall rise. No power can hold in durance the redeemed of the Lord. "Let my people go" shall be a command as much obeyed by death as once by the humbled Pharaoh who could not hold a single Israelite in bonds. The day of deliverance cometh on apace.

> " Break from His throne, illustrious morn!
> Attend, O earth, His sovereign word;
> Restore thy trust, a glorious form:
> He must ascend to meet his Lord."

Once more, *our Lord's rising from the dead is a fair picture of the new life which all believers already enjoy.* Beloved, though this body is still subject to bondage like the rest of the visible creation, according to the law stated in Scripture, "the body is dead because of sin," yet "the spirit is life because of righteousness." The regeneration which has taken place in those who believe has changed our spirit, and given to it eternal life, but it has not affected our body further than this, that it has made it to be the temple of the Holy Ghost, and thus it is a holy thing, and cannot be obnoxious to the Lord, or swept away among unholy things; but still the body is subject to pain and weariness, and to the supreme sentence of death. Not so the spirit. There is within us already a part of the resurrection accomplished, since it is written, "And you hath he quickened who were dead in trespasses and sins." You once were like the ungodly, under the law of sin and death, but you have been brought out of the bondage of corruption into the liberty of life and grace; the Lord having wrought in you gloriously, "according to the working of his mighty power, which he wrought in Christ, when He raised Him from the dead, and set Him at His own right hand in the heavenly places."

Now, just as Jesus Christ led, after His resurrection, a life very different from that before His death, so you and I are called upon to live a high and noble spiritual and heavenly life, seeing that we have been raised from the dead to die no more. Let us joy and rejoice in this. Let us behave as those who are alive from the dead, the happy children of the resurrection. Do not let us be money-grubbers, or hunters after worldly fame. Let us not set our affections on the foul things of this dead and rotten world, but let our hearts fly upward, like young birds that have broken loose of their shells—upward towards our Lord and the heavenly things upon which He would have us set our minds. Living truth, living work, living faith, these are the things for living men: let us cast off the graveclothes of our former lusts, and wear the garments of light and life. May the Spirit of God help us in further meditating upon these things at home.

II. Now, secondly, LET US CONSIDER THE BEARINGS OF THIS FACT OF THE RESURRECTION UPON THE GOSPEL; for Paul says, "Jesus Christ was raised from the dead *according to my gospel*." I always like to see what way any kind of statement bears on the gospel. I may not have many more opportunities of preaching, and I make up my mind to this one thing, that I will waste no time upon secondary themes, but when I do preach it shall be the gospel, or something very closely bearing upon it. I will endeavour each time to strike under the fifth rib, and never beat the air. Some preachers remind me of the emperor who had a wonderful skill in carving men's heads upon cherry stones. What a multitude of preachers we have who can make wonderfully fine discourses out of a mere passing thought, of no consequence to anyone. But we want the gospel. We have to live and die, and we must have the gospel. Certain of us may be cold in our graves before many weeks are over, and we cannot afford to toy and trifle: we want to see the bearings of all teachings upon our eternal destinies, and upon the gospel which sheds its light over our future.

The resurrection of Christ is vital, because first it tells us that *the gospel is the gospel of a living Saviour*. We have not to send poor penitents to the crucifix, the dead image of a dead man. We say not, "These be thy gods, O Israel!" We have not to send you to a little baby Christ nursed by a woman. Nothing of the sort. Behold the Lord that liveth and was dead and is alive for evermore, and hath the keys of hell and of death! Behold in Him a living and accessible Saviour who out of the glory still cries with loving accents, "Come unto me, all ye that labour and are heavy laden, and I will give you rest." "He is able also to save them to the uttermost that come unto God by him, seeing he ever liveth to make intercession for them." I say we have a living Saviour, and is not this a glorious feature of the gospel?

Notice next that *we have a powerful Saviour* in connection with the gospel that we preach; for He Who had power to raise Himself from the dead, has all power now that He is raised. He Who in death vanquishes death, can much more conquer by His life. He Who being in the grave did, nevertheless, burst all its bonds, can assuredly deliver all His people. He Who, coming under the power of the law, did, nevertheless, fulfil the law, and thus set His people free from bondage, must be mighty to save. You need a Saviour strong and mighty, yet you do not want one stronger than He of Whom it is written that He rose again from the dead. What a blessed gospel we have to preach,— the gospel of a living Christ Who hath Himself returned from the dead leading captivity captive.

And now notice, that we have *the gospel of complete justification* to preach to you. We do not come and say, "Brethren, Jesus Christ by His death did something by which men may be saved if they have a mind to be, and diligently carry out their good resolves." No, no; we say Jesus Christ took the sin of His people upon Himself and bore the consequences of it in His own body on the tree, so that He died; and having died, and so paid the penalty, He lives again; and now all for whom He died, all His people whose sins He bore, are free from the guilt of sin. You ask me, "Who are they?" and I reply, as many as believe on Him. Whosoever believeth in Jesus Christ is as free from the guilt of sin as Christ is. Our Lord Jesus took the sin of His people, and died in the sinner's stead, and now being Himself set free, all His people are set free in their Representative. He has performed the work entrusted to Him. He has finished transgression, made an end of sin, and brought in everlasting righteousness, and whosoever believeth in Him is not condemned, and never can be.

Once again, the connection of the resurrection and the gospel is this, *it proves the safety of the saints*, for if when Christ rose His people rose also, they rose to a life like that of their Lord, and therefore they can never die. It is written, "Christ being raised from the dead dieth no more; death hath no more dominion over him," and it is so with the believer: if you have been dead with Christ and are risen with Christ, death has no more dominion over you; you shall never go back to the beggarly elements of sin, you shall never become what you were before your regeneration. You shall never perish, neither shall any pluck you out of Jesus' hand. He has put within you a living and incorruptible seed which liveth and abideth for ever. He says Himself, "The water that I shall give him shall be in him a well of living water springing up unto everlasting life." Wherefore hold ye fast to this, and let the resurrection of your Lord be the pledge of your own final perseverance.

Brethren, I cannot stop to show you how this resurrection touches the gospel at every point, but Paul is always full of it. More than thirty times Paul talks about the resurrection, and occasionally at great length, giving whole chapters to the glorious theme. The more I think of it the more I delight to preach Jesus and the resurrection. The glad tidings that Christ has risen is as truly the gospel as the doctrine that He came among men and for men presented His blood as a ransom. If angels sang glory to God in the highest when the Lord was born, I feel impelled to repeat the note now that He is risen from the dead.

III. And so I come to my last head, and to the practical conclusion: THE BEARING OF THIS RESURRECTION UPON OURSELVES. Paul expressly bids us "Remember" it. "Why," says one, "we don't forget it." Are you sure you do not? I find myself far too forgetful of divine truths. We ought not to forget, for this first day of the week is consecrated for Sabbatic purposes to constrain us to think of the resurrection. On the seventh day men celebrated a finished creation, on the first day we celebrate a finished redemption. Bear it, then, in mind. Now, if you will remember that Jesus Christ of the seed of David rose from the dead, what will follow?

First, you will find that *most of your trials will vanish*. Are you tried by your sin? Jesus Christ rose again from the dead for your justification. Does Satan accuse? Jesus rose to be your advocate and intercessor. Do infirmities hinder? The living Christ will show Himself strong on your behalf. You have a living Christ, and in Him you have all things. Do you dread death? Jesus in rising again, has vanquished the last enemy. He will come and meet you when it is your turn to pass through the chill stream, and you shall ford it in sweet company. What is your trouble? I care not what it is, for if you will only think of Jesus as living, full of power, full of love, and full of sympathy, having experienced all your trials, even unto death, you will have such a confidence in His tender care and in His boundless ability that you will follow in His footsteps without a question. Remember Jesus, and that He rose again from the dead, and your confidence will rise as on eagles' wings.

Next remember Jesus, for then you will see how your present sufferings are as nothing compared with His sufferings, and you will learn to *expect victory over your sufferings even as He obtained victory*. Kindly look at the chapter, and you will find the apostle there saying in the third verse, "Thou therefore endure hardness, as a good soldier of Jesus Christ," and further on in the eleventh verse, "It is a faithful saying: For if we be dead in him, we shall also live in him: if we suffer, we shall also reign with him." Now, then, when you are called to suffer, think,—"Jesus suffered, yet Jesus rose again from the dead; He came up out of His baptism of griefs the better and more glorious for it, and so shall I!" Wherefore go you into the furnace at the Lord's bidding, and do not fear that the smell of fire shall pass upon you. Go you even down into the grave, and do not think that the worm shall make an end of you any more than it did of Him. Behold in the risen One the type and model of what you are to be! Wherefore fear not, for He conquered! Stand not trembling, but march boldly on, for Jesus Christ of the seed of David rose from the dead, and you who are of the seed of the promise shall rise again from all your trials and afflictions and live a glorious life.

We see here, dear brethren, in being told to remember Jesus that *there is hope even in our hopelessness*. When are things most hopeless in a man? Why, when he is dead. Do you know what it is to come down to that, so far as your inward weakness is concerned? I do. We take a deal of killing, and it is by being killed that we live. Many a man will never live till his proud self is slain. Alas, how many are so good and excellent, and strong and wise, and clever, and all that, that they cannot agree to be saved by grace through faith. If they could be reduced to less than nothing it would be the finest thing that ever happened to them. Remember what Solomon said might be done with the fool, and yet it would not answer—he was to be brayed in a mortar among wheat with a pestle,—pretty hard dealing that, and yet his folly would not depart from him. Not by that process alone, but through some such method, the Holy Spirit brings men away from their folly. Under His killing operations this may be their comfort that, if Jesus Christ rose literally from the dead (not from sickness, but from death), and lives again, even so will His people.

Did you ever get, where Bunyan pictures Christian as getting, right under the old dragon's foot? He is very heavy, and presses the very breath out of a fellow when he makes him his footstool. Poor Christian lay there with the dragon's foot on his breast; but he was just able to stretch out his hand and lay hold on his sword, which, by a good providence, lay within his reach. Then he gave Apollyon a deadly thrust, which made him spread his dragon wings and fly away. The poor crushed and broken pilgrim, as he gave the stab to his foe, cried, "Rejoice not over me, O mine enemy; though I fall, yet shall I rise again." Brother, do you the same. You that are near despair, let this be the strength that nerves your arm and steels your heart. "Jesus Christ of the seed of David was raised from the dead according to Paul's gospel."

Lastly, this proves *the futility of all opposition to Christ*. The learned are going to destroy the Christian religion. Already, according to their boastings, it has pretty nearly come to an end. The pulpit is effete, it cannot command public attention. We stand up and preach to empty benches! As you see—*or do not see*. Nothing remains for us but to die decently, so they insinuate. And what then? When our Lord was dead, when the clay-cold corpse lay, watched by the Roman soldiery, and with a seal upon the enclosing stone, was not the cause in mortal jeopardy? But how fared it? Did it die out? Every disciple that Jesus had made forsook Him, and fled, was not Christianity then destroyed? Nay, that very day our Lord won a victory which shook the gates of hell, and caused the universe to stand astonished. Matters are not worse with Him at this hour! His affairs are not in a sadder condition to-day than then. Nay, see Him to-day and judge. On His head are many crowns, and at His feet the hosts of angels bow! Jesus is the master of legions to-day, while the Cæsars have passed away! Here are His people—needy, obscure, despised, I grant you, still, but assuredly somewhat more numerous than they were when they laid Him in the tomb. His cause is not to be crushed, it is for ever rising. Year after year, century after century, bands of true and honest hearts are marching up to the assault of the citadel of Satan.

Truly if Christ were dead I would admit our defeat, for they that are fallen asleep in Him would have perished: but as the Christ liveth so the cause liveth, and they that have fallen are not dead: they have vanished from our sight for a little, but if the curtain could be withdrawn every one of them would be seen to stand in his lot unharmed, crowned, victorious! "Who are these arrayed in white robes, and whence came they?" These are they that were defeated! Whence, then, their crowns? These are they that were dishonoured! Whence then their white robes? These are they who clung to a cause which is overthrown. Whence then their long line of victors, for there is not a vanquished man among them all?

Let the truth be spoken. Defeat is not the word for the cause of Jesus, the Prince of the house of David. We have always been victorious, brethren; we are victorious now. Follow your Master on your white horses, and be not afraid! I see Him in the front with His blood-stained vesture around Him, fresh from the wine-press where He has trodden down His foes. You have not to present atoning blood, but only to conquer after your Lord. Put on your white raiment and follow Him on your white horses,. conquering and to conquer. He is nearer than we think, and the end of all things may be before the next jibe shall have come forth from the mouth of the last new sceptic. Have confidence in the risen One, and live in the power of His resurrection.